THE RETREAT TO COMMITMENT

THE
RETREAT
TO
COMMITMENT

BY

William Warren Bartley III

ALFRED · A · KNOPF : *New York*

1 9 6 2

L. C. catalog card number: 62–8674

THIS IS A BORZOI BOOK,
PUBLISHED BY ALFRED A. KNOPF, INC.

FIRST EDITION

TO MY MOTHER

Elvina Henry Bartley

THERE IS NOBODY *in the common-wealth of learning who does not profess himself a lover of truth; and there is not a rational creature that would not take it amiss to be thought otherwise of. And yet, for all this, one may truly say, there are very few lovers of truth for truth's sake, even amongst those who persuade themselves that they are so. How a man may know whether he be so in earnest, is worth enquiry.*

JOHN LOCKE, 1699

PREFACE

THIS is an essay in the theory of the open mind. Through a study of the conflict between the rationalist and Protestant traditions it tries to solve what has been called "the central problem that confronts moral philosophers in our time." [1] This problem, which lies at the core of that conflict, is whether some form of relativist existentialism is inescapable because rationality is so limited, logically as well as practically, that the choice between ultimately competing religious, moral, and philosophical positions is, in the last resort, *arbitrary*. For example, is an individual's decision to become a *rationalist*—even from a rationalist point of view—any less subjective, relative, arbitrary, irrational than an individual's decision to become a Christian?

Not surprisingly, concern with this problem, and with the clash between competing traditions, often arises out of personal conflict. Bertrand Russell, one of the most ardent contemporary apostles of the Enlightenment, seems to pro-

[1] D. H. Munro: "Russell's Moral Theories," *Philosophy*, January 1960, p. 50.

vide a case in point. Not long ago, writing about the implications of moral relativism, he said:

> I am not, myself, satisfied with what I have read or said on the philosophical basis of ethics. I cannot see how to refute the arguments for the subjectivity of ethical values, but I find myself incapable of believing that all that is wrong with wanton cruelty is that I don't like it. . . . when it comes to the philosophy of moral judgments, I am impelled in two opposite directions and remain perplexed. I should deeply rejoice, if I could find or be shown a way to resolve this perplexity, but as yet I remain dissatisfied.[2]

The answer to the problem of this essay—I shall refer to it alternatively as the dilemma of ultimate commitment and as the problem of the limits of rationality—is of fundamental importance in any attempt to resolve such perplexity. For if relativism is inescapable, then a consistent rational liberalism becomes intellectually impossible.

Throughout his life, Kierkegaard sought to answer the question: How can I become a Christian? Barely two generations later, Nietzsche sought to learn how men could live as atheists in a world where God was dead. There is something of both these questions in the following pages. But the main question, a question that expresses the principal philosophical interest of many persons today, is this: How is it possible any longer for a man to remain a con-

[2] Bertrand Russell: "Notes on *Philosophy*, January 1960," *Philosophy*, April 1960.

sistent liberal rationalist? The Enlightenment seems to have come to that.[3]

In the following pages I intend to show that it is *untrue* that the choice between competing moral, religious, political, or philosophical creeds—such as Christianity, Communism, and empiricism—must be fundamentally irrational. My conclusions involve a proposal about the essence or identity not of Christianity but of rationality, or the tradition of rational discussion; a proposal that rejects most traditional and contemporary characterizations.

A word about the essay's many limitations. Since my main efforts have been to understand a philosophical problem, to present the outline of its solution, and to indicate some of the consequences within the Protestant and rationalist traditions of the belief that the problem could not be solved, my historical and social observations, most of them drawn from American life and thought, are used only as examples and illustrations which are intended to lend context and clarity to the main argument. I do not pretend to give an exhaustive critique of the thinkers or the systems

[3] Several senses of the word "rationalism" are in common circulation. In one sense it is used to refer to the predominantly seventeenth-century rationalist (as opposed to empiricist) thought of philosophers like Descartes, Spinoza, and Leibniz. But the term may also be used to refer, in the most general way, to the tradition whose members are dedicated to the task of trying to learn more about the world through the practice of critical argument. I shall use the term in the second sense throughout this essay, one of my main aims being to make this sense more precise. I follow many writers in using the term "intellectualism" for the first sense. Neither kind of rationalism necessarily involves another view that is sometimes called "rationalism," the undoubtedly false view that men are able to act rationally most or all of the time.

of thought which I discuss and criticize. The published work of the most important Protestant theologian, Karl Barth, alone runs to over 15,000 printed pages of rather small type—even though he once described much of his work as a "footnote" to theology. I have tried to aim my criticisms at only the most basic assumptions of these systems of thought, their feet as it were, without which they cannot stand.

W. W. B.

St. John's Wood
LONDON

ACKNOWLEDGMENTS

I HAVE BEEN grappling for a long time with the issues treated in this essay, and owe a word of thanks to my teachers. I am especially grateful to my undergraduate tutor at Harvard College, Raphael Demos, who introduced me to the problems of philosophy, and to my graduate supervisor, Morton White, who first inspired me to become a teacher of philosophy.

Most of all I am indebted to my great teacher and friend Karl R. Popper, of the London School of Economics and Political Science. I believe that Professor Popper has succeeded, whereas Kant failed, in solving Kant's problem—to reconcile and explain the valid elements of both intellectualism and empiricism while avoiding the mistakes of each. More important, I believe that he has presented the first example in the history of philosophy of what I shall later call a "nonjustificational philosophy of criticism." Although I do not agree with everything he has said or written, I believe that his thought is no less than epoch-making and would be proud to think that its impact has influenced every page of this essay. In addition to ideas he has presented in his books, the concepts of three of his papers have been very much in my mind as I wrote. These are: "Towards a Rational Theory of Tradition," "Back to the Pre-Socratics," and "On the Sources of Knowledge and of Ignorance." [1] The latter, in particular, is discussed in chapter V. I am also deeply indebted to Professor Popper for many exciting conversations on these and related matters.

It is a pleasure to thank Joseph Agassi, Nels F. S. Ferré, I. C. Jarvie, Walter Kaufmann, S. C. Parikh, Leroy S. Rouner, H. Hugh Van Dusen, and J. W. N. Watkins, who have criticized an earlier draft of this essay. Although their comments have helped me to make major improvements, they are of course in no way responsible for the mistakes that remain; in several cases they have disagreed emphatically with me. I am particularly indebted to Mr. Kaufmann and Mr. Watkins, whose painstaking criticisms have saved me from a number of blunders and forced me to rewrite several parts of the essay.

I also want to thank Jeffrey A. Barach, Imre Lakatos, and J. C. Peter Richardson for the benefit of personal conversation about some of the topics discussed here, and my students at the London School of Economics and at the Royal Institute of Philosophy for their keen interest and for the questions they raised in my courses in moral philosophy, where I applied some of the ideas of this book to contemporary ethical theory. I am also indebted to my seminar students at the Austrian College, Alpbach, Tirol, for their unusually stimulating discussion of the implications of my argument in the philosophy of science.

[1] Printed, respectively, in *The Rationalist Annual*, 1949; *The Proceedings of the Aristotelian Society*, 1958–9; and *The Proceedings of the British Academy*, 1960.

I wish to thank M. J. C. Ellis for help with the proofs and for compiling the index.

I am grateful to Harvard University, the United States Educational Commission in the United Kingdom, and the Danforth Foundation for fellowships which enabled me to work on the problems of the book.

                                              W. W. B.

The Warburg Institute
University of London

CONTENTS

THE RETREAT TO COMMITMENT

Identity, Integrity, and Commitment to Confusion

WHOEVER is hard put to feel identical with one set of people and ideas must that much more violently repudiate another set; and whenever an identity, once established, meets further crises, the danger of irrational repudiation of otherness and temporarily even of one's own identity increases.

ERIK H. ERIKSON, 1958 [1]

I MUST earnestly beg the kind reader always to bear in mind that the thought behind the whole work is: what it means to become a Christian . . . the truth and inwardness of the reflective expression for becoming a Christian is measured by the value of the thing which reflection is bound to reject . . . one does not reflect oneself into being a Christian, but out of another thing in order to become a Christian. . . . The nature of the other thing decides how deep, how significant, the movement of reflection is. . . . The reflection is defined by the difficulty, which is greater just in proportion to the value of the thing left behind.

SØREN KIERKEGAARD, 1848 [2]

ONE of the commonest complaints about the present might be expressed in this way: ours is a time when the rebel with-

[1] Erik H. Erikson: *Young Man Luther* (New York: W. W. Norton & Company; 1958), p. 259.

[2] Søren Kierkegaard: *The Point of View for My Work as an Author*, written in 1848 and first published posthumously in 1859, four years after the author's death.

out a cause has succeeded the rebel without an effect. Whereas our ancestors, even when they strove in vain, seemed to know what they were against and what they were for, we see good and bad in everything and rebel against our state of indecision. Unable to find purpose in our lives, we hold symposia on "national purpose." Our literature and social commentary and even our manners are composed out of the vocabulary of alienation: "indifference," "withdrawal," "disenchantment," "non-involvement," and "No, thanks" spell the distance between contemporary men and future ideals as well as old loyalties.

Like most such complaints, this one denigrates the present at the expense of idealizing the past. Yet despite this, and despite its hackneyed character, it is both apt and timely. For people are not yet alienated from the problem of alienation, nor indifferent to the hope of overcoming indifference. Although one social analyst has claimed that "the *direction* of cultural change is from commitment and enthusiasm to alienation and apathy," [3] alienation is still treated as an urgent *problem,* to be ameliorated if not overcome, not as something like death which must be helplessly accepted. This very involvement with indifference perhaps explains in part why the phenomena and mood of alienation uneasily coexist with an obsession—in religion, politics, literature, philosophy—with those things that once were thought to diminish alienation: ideology and commitment. "Obsession" is not too strong a word. For even in academic philosophy, often proudly claimed by its practitioners to be one of the most abstract and impractical of subjects,

[3] See Kenneth Kenniston's sensitive discussion, "Alienation and the Decline of Utopia," *American Scholar,* Spring 1960, p. 162.

the related notions of "commitment," "choice," and "decision" have forced their way to the center of discussion—and
this on both sides of the Atlantic, in movements as differ-
ently rooted as the British philosophy of linguistic analysis
and contemporary American pragmatism.[4] In the more
popularly directed French and German philosophies, the
same notions are motifs for the various existentialisms.

Ardor for commitment, however, rarely seems to be adequate by itself to overcome alienation. It is true that many
people, baffled about who they are and what they might be
or should be, and incapable of forging acceptable personali-
ties for themselves, still try to bring order into their lives
by choosing ready-made characters and causes—by identifying, sometimes through what is called a "free commitment," with some established cultural tradition. However,
regardless of the country or philosophical tradition in which
they are made, these commitments have a way of waning
—particularly among those who seem most in need of
them. Migration from one "absolute" commitment to another, although occasionally constricted by social sanction,
is largely unrestricted. Divorcing one's commitment—apart
from the comparatively rare political case—requires no legal
proceedings, even when it is attended with as much psychological turmoil as divorcing one's wife. The ideological

---

[4] For examples out of an extensive literature, see these essays and books,
the first group by an eminent British philosopher, the second by an eminent
American: Stuart Hampshire: "Identification and Existence," *Contemporary British Philosophy*, ed. H. D. Lewis (New York: The Macmillan
Company; 1956), and *Thought and Action* (London: Chatto and Windus;
1959); Morton White: *Toward Reunion in Philosophy* (Cambridge:
Harvard University Press; 1956), pp. 231 ff, 272 ff, and Chap. XVI; and
Religion, Politics, and the Higher Learning (Cambridge: Harvard University Press; 1959), Chap. IV (2) and X.

divorcing and remarrying; the uneasiness of many who remain "settled down"; and the tensions of those who never
wed again or at all—all are themselves part of the situation of alienation.

If the estrangement from cause and commitment helps
to explain the fruitless yet fervid experimentation in just
such cause and commitment, what explains the alienation
in the first place? It is difficult to say. The situation is probably too complex to lend itself to a compact or simple explanation.

Nonetheless, I believe that one important source of the
situation, and—more particularly—of the seemingly en-
demic frustration that meets those "cultural physicians"
who attempt to correct it, has been almost entirely unex-
plored. What I have in mind is this. We are faced today by
a circumstance that radically limits the effectiveness of any
personal or social cause, aim, identification, or commitment
from the very start. Namely, *the most important of the traditions in which identity, purpose, and commitment have
been sought themselves partake in the general confusion.*
Traditions, too, appear not only to have been evolving but
to have been going through agonizing self-analysis and to
have emerged lacking an inner core. Thus the man who
tries to acquire a character or a cause by identifying himself, through commitment, with a particular tradition often exchanges his "I am confused" for an "I am a member
of a confused tradition." Doubtless he may gain thereby,
at least temporarily, in personal happiness: now he has a
name; he can at least say what he is. But he cannot so easily
explain what it is to be what he is, not so much because he
does not know as because no one knows, or else because

everyone has a different answer.[5] This is one reason why mysticism accompanies so many commitments.

This situation of internal confusion in those traditions within whose resources we might have expected to find identity has sometimes been obscured, partly because traditions are often wrongly represented as blocklike social entities, secure against change; partly because the demand for suitable characters has sometimes outstripped the supply of available traditions, with the result that simple substitutes have appeared, complete with brand names and labeled contents, to entice speculators in commitment. The situation looks different, however, as soon as we turn from such manufactured items—particularly from those like Nazism [6] which make little pretense of being rationally defensible—to the older, intellectually and morally more serious traditions, such as rationalistic humanism, Christianity, or even, to a lesser extent, Communism. Few of those who are spiritually committed to Christianity, for instance, could describe its "essence," let alone defend it. "Who can tell what vagary or what compromise may not be calling itself Christianity?" asked Santayana more than fifty years ago. "A bishop may be a modernist, a chemist may be a mystical theologian, a psychologist may be a believer in ghosts." [7] Santayana was observing, not complaining. After all, he described himself as both an atheist and a Roman

[5] For an interesting discussion of some related questions, see Van A. Harvey: "On Believing What Is Difficult to Understand," *Journal of Religion*, October 1959.

[6] Or anti-Semitism. See Jean-Paul Sartre: "Portrait of the Anti-Semite," *Partisan Review*, Spring 1946.

[7] George Santayana: *Winds of Doctrine* (New York: Harper and Brothers; 1957), p. 4.

Catholic. What Santayana believes, someone jibed, is that "there is no God, and Mary is His Mother."

When Santayana wrote this passage, the papal encyclical *Pascendi Dominici Gregis,* of September 8, 1907—which had exorcised Catholic modernism while assigning the blame for it to "curiosity and pride"—was still a mildly controversial document. Today, however, the modernism controversy in Roman Catholicism has, for practical purposes, long been silenced. To be a Catholic Christian is, at the very least, to accept the authority of the Pope in certain matters of faith and morals. On the other hand, the situation in Protestant Christianity is even murkier today than it was in 1910. If, indeed, as has been suggested, a *tradition,* which is marked by a relative uniformity of attitudes, ways of behavior, aims, and values, may be distinguished from an institution, which merely fulfills certain social functions for shifting groups of very different people,[8] then Protestantism is becoming less a tradition than an institution. For being a Protestant now seems to require little more than calling oneself a Protestant, and finding it helpful, spiritually, socially, or in some other way, to do so. What is "generally lacking," as Kierkegaard insisted more than a hundred years ago, is a "decisive categorical definition" for a situation in which "one does not know and cannot make out whether one is situated in paganism, whether the parson is a missionary in that sense, or whereabouts one is." [9]

Today, Kierkegaard's question of what it is to be a Christian has become an almost obsessive preoccupation of Prot-

[8] Karl R. Popper: "Towards a Rational Theory of Tradition," *Rationalist Annual,* 1949, pp. 52–4.

[9] Kierkegaard: op. cit.

estant Christians. For during the last thirty years, Protestant thought, both rejecting and rejected by the groups and traditions with which it had been allied and from which it had drawn nourishment throughout its history, has had to face the choice of either forging for itself a newly independent identity, more secure against the betrayal of unreliable allies, or else of abdicating the claim to authority and even to leadership in intellectual or spiritual matters. For Protestantism, this was tantamount to a choice between irrationalism and suicide.

This essay is a study of problems of self-identity and integrity in the Protestant and rationalist traditions. Probably the two most influential spiritual traditions of our culture, both have helped provide involvement and purposive living in the past; and both still offer their services to help overcome present-day alienation. However, these two traditions not only are internally confused but are breeding confusion and alienation quite out of proportion to the internal confusion of either. Their identities are so intertwined historically that members of either (the rationalist as well as the Protestant Christian) must try to understand the nature of their own tradition partly by contrasting it with the identity of the other. So confusion in one engenders confusion in the other.

I shall approach these matters, and try to clarify them, in terms of a study of the relationship of the present *crisis of identity* in Protestantism to a long-standing *crisis of integrity* in the rationalist tradition.

Problems connected with identity and integrity are of course very familiar. I intend to use these two ideas, and in

particular the two phrases just italicized, in a sense I bor-
row from the sociologist and psychoanalyst Erik H. Erikson.[1] They refer to two characteristic turning points in the
lives of most individuals, periods which particularly in the
life of the *homo religiosus*, be he priest or philosopher, are
often fused.[2] The individual's problem of identity, encountered by most people in late adolescence and early adult-
hood, is to shape, out of the elements provided by his heritage, his conception of himself, and his idea of what others
see in him, an identity that he believes he will be able to
live with in integrity. The problem of integrity is, given
one's identity, purpose, and claims about oneself, how to
live up to them.

Although these concepts are primarily intended to refer
to periods in the lives of individual human beings, they
can be usefully applied, provided we are careful, to such
things as traditions and societies. Since the application of
such concepts to "social wholes" is a procedure fraught with
danger, a word of caution is in order here. To say that a society or tradition is involved in a crisis of identity is not to
make a profoundly mysterious statement or to claim, for
instance, that "the collective consciousness" is on the verge
of a nervous collapse. To illustrate: when we transfer these
concepts from individuals to traditions we must leave behind part of the original theory. In individual human beings, crises of identity typically occur in late adolescence. To
traditions, however, which are not biological organisms, the

---

[1] Erikson: *Childhood and Society* (London: Imago Publishing Co.;
1950); *Young Man Luther*, p. 14 *passim*; and *Identity and the Life Cycle*,
Psychological Issues, Monograph 1, 1959.
[2] See *Young Man Luther*, p. 261.

concept of adolescence does not apply.[3] I shall use these
concepts as shorthand devices for indicating that the individual thinkers and writers of the traditions in question,
those who attempt to evaluate them and make articulate
their fundamental characteristics, are baffled by their job,
and that this bafflement extends to those who look to them
as spiritual guides.

In outline, my thesis is this. Despite a chronic crisis of
identity, which has suddenly in this century become acute,
it has been still possible to identify with the Protestant tradition while retaining intellectual integrity. However, this
is so only because of the existence of an unanswered philosophical argument that has made it impossible for adherents of the *rationalist* tradition to live in genuine integrity
with their own self-image or identity. The same philosophical argument, in many respects a logical puzzle, provides at
once a wanted refuge of safety for Protestants and a skele-
ton in the rationalists' intellectual closet. Rationalists are
overcommitted to a notion of rationality that is impossible
to attain; and the seemingly inevitable frustration of the
effort to escape this overcommitment prevents them from
achieving integrity.

The failure of rationalists to resolve their own crisis of
integrity—a failure which, in turn, is rooted in their own
problems of identity—has enabled Protestants to preserve
their Protestant identity without loss of integrity.

[3] Perhaps the main error of "sociological holism," which is a name for
the application to social wholes, such as societies and civilizations, of
concepts that originate in the description of human behavior, may be
generalized, in a pun, as follows. The error of holism is the *wholesale*
transfer of such concepts from human beings to social wholes. In fact,
some may be transferred and some may not.

However, if the rationalist crisis of integrity could be resolved—if it were possible to answer the philosophical argument in which it is rooted—then it would no longer be
possible for a man to retain his Protestant identity with
intellectual integrity. A Protestant could no longer contend
that "since rationality, or critical activity, is fundamentally
limited," Protestant Christian faith can legitimately
come in when that limit is reached.

In the course of this essay I hope to explain my thesis, to
probe the inner resources of the contemporary Protestant
identity, and then to resolve the crisis of integrity of the rationalist tradition by solving the problem of the limits of
rationality, thereby eliminating this rational excuse for
Protestant commitment. To achieve these aims, we must
begin by considering the background and the outcome of
the search for identity in both Protestantism and rationalism. These two traditions interacted most significantly in
recent history in the period of the breakdown of Protestant
liberalism and the resultant shift to neo-orthodox thought.

I I

THE
Search for Identity
in Protestantism

DURING the last year or two, few weeks have gone by when some liberal chieftain has not passed down the national thoroughfare of one or another of our high-grade and more highly circulated periodicals noisily scourging his idol. . . . speculation grows on "after liberalism what?" A new idol is expected to appear presently and the curious are occupying themselves with imaginative anticipation.

J. C. DANCEY, 1934 [1]

BECAUSE I have been and am a modernist it is proper that I should confess that often the modernistic movement, adjusting itself to a man-centered culture, has . . . watered down the thought of the Divine and, may we be forgiven for this, left souls standing like the ancient Athenians, before an altar to an Unknown God! On that point the church must go beyond modernism. We have been all things to all men long enough. We have adapted and adjusted and accommodated and conceded long enough. We have at times gotten so low down that we talked as though the highest compliment that could be paid to Almighty God was that a few scientists believed in him. Yet all the time, by right, we had an independent standing ground and a message of our own in which alone is there hope for humankind.

HARRY EMERSON FOSDICK, 1935 [2]

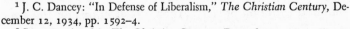

[1] J. C. Dancey: "In Defense of Liberalism," *The Christian Century*, December 12, 1934, pp. 1592–4.

[2] Sermon printed in *The Christian Century*, December 4, 1935.

1 · *The New Idol*

In the autumn of 1935, when Harry Emerson Fosdick climbed to his pulpit in Riverside Church to denounce the excesses of modernist Protestant liberalism, much of the conflict, irony, and pathos of twentieth-century American religion surely came together. In this lopsided, "nondenominational Baptist," neo-Gothic cathedral overlooking Riverside Drive on one side and Harlem on the other, buttressed from within by steel girders, paid for by the Rockefeller family, and echoing with the strains of old-fashioned hymns piped out by a kind of glorified music-hall organ, the leading preacher of Protestant liberalism—a man who had been attacked by many of his fellow Christians during half his life because of his "betrayal" of genuine Christianity—was about to confess to his prosperous congregation that his own brand of modernist liberalism had gone too far, that he was now joining those who required a more distinctly Christian gospel.

Fosdick's sermon in itself marked no watershed of thinking; it simply dramatized a trend. By the time he spoke out, the features of the new idol that was to replace Protestant liberalism in the new world as well as in the old were becoming clear. Paul Tillich, who had arrived in New York City in November 1933, a refugee from Hitler's Germany, had begun to publish his first articles in English. Reinhold Niebuhr—like Tillich, a colleague of Fosdick's at Union Theological Seminary, on New York City's Morningside Heights—had published in quick succession his *Moral Man and Immoral Society* (1932), *Reflections on the End of an Era* (1934), and *An Interpretation of Christian*

Ethics (1935),[3] three books that were to make Niebuhr's original reinterpretation and application of some ideas of Karl Barth and Emil Brunner familiar to the American public, and to help change the climate of religious thought in the United States. In 1925 Niebuhr had asked: "Shall we proclaim the truth or search for it?" [4] A decade later, he was enjoining Christians and liberals to "stop fooling themselves," [5] and proclaiming "the pathos of liberalism." [6]

The new idol that was to replace liberalism is referred to by names like "neo-orthodoxy," and "new Reformation theology." Although the emphases of this new theology have changed considerably in the last twenty-five years, its main themes remain largely the same, and its leading figures are still Barth, Brunner, Niebuhr, and Tillich. These themes are suggested both by the names of the movement and by Fosdick's address. The movement is new, and yet connected somehow with the orthodox Protestant theology of the Reformation. Opposed to liberalism and to the undignified "adjustment and accommodation" that attended liberal theology, it stresses the importance of an "independent standing ground" or "impregnable stronghold" [7] for Christianity. And it is led not by thinkers with backgrounds in fundamentalism but by men like Fosdick, liberal in tendency, alive to change. At the same time, Fosdick's

[3] The first two were published by Charles Scribner's Sons, of New York; and the last by Harper & Brothers, of New York.

[4] *The Christian Century*, March 12, 1925, pp. 344–6.

[5] "When Will Christians Stop Fooling Themselves?" *The Christian Century*, May 16, 1934, pp. 658–60. See also "Let Liberal Churches Stop Fooling Themselves!" *The Christian Century*, March 25, 1931.

[6] *The Nation*, September 11, 1935, pp. 303–4.

[7] Karl Heim: *Christian Faith and Natural Science* (New York: Harper and Brothers; 1957), pp. 32–3.

address also suggests the variety of the opinions united under the antiliberal banner. For example, although one of Barth's main theses was that the Christian God was indeed "Unknown," [8] Fosdick prayed for divine forgiveness for this very idea.

2 · A Logical Development

This new Protestant thought is complicated. Yet accounts of it are often oversimplified, especially by the type of critic who tries to explain it away as little more than a religious echo of the social, moral, and intellectual evils and upheavals of the twentieth century. There is more exaggeration than truth in such interpretations.

It is, to be sure, one of the ironies of modern thought that the existence of evil—the biggest problem and greatest embarrassment of the eighteenth-century theologians—has become one of the most persuasive argumentative assets of their twentieth-century successors. Contemporary religious apologia often begin by calling one's attention to the disunity and misery of the present world, continue by attacking for its superficiality some popular theory that does not emphasize the existence of such woe, and proceed to exult that Christianity (as if it were the only alternative) has always recognized the ambiguous nature of man and the existence of sin in the world. Acceptance of Christianity and abandonment of the alternative theory are urged as the answers to the evil—whatever the evil, the theory, or the interpretation of Christianity happens to be.

This strategy has great persuasive power and rhetorical

[8] See also the final chapter of H. R. Niebuhr: *Christ and Culture* (New York: Harper and Brothers; 1956).

effectiveness: there is nothing like evil, especially when described in a rather lurid way with statistics on suicides, war
tolls, mental-hospital enrollment, and the destructive
power of nuclear weapons, to set the mood for the acceptance of a *non sequitur*. It is not surprising, then, that many
people have found the *non sequitur* more tolerable than the
misery and meaninglessness. To accept a *non sequitur* is, of
course, to contravene the logical rules of valid argument,
and perhaps to try

> . . . *to arrange a private validity*
> *And make nature envious of what*
> *She so deplorably undervalues.*[9]

Is contemporary theology, then—like the products of
many other *non sequiturs*—no more than an understandable neurosis, an imaginary foxhole dug in no man's land,
something the theologians have invented in order to cope
with the unbearable reality around them? The question of
the origin of contemporary theology, as well as the question of its truth, must be separated from the question of its
popularity. Although it is true that the basic defense of
contemporary Protestant thought ultimately rests on an appeal to irrationalism, many of the most significant features
of its historical development are fairly logical products of
certain long-standing theological assumptions, combined
with those conclusions of late nineteenth- and early twentieth-century Biblical criticism and social and political
thinking which made Protestant liberalism untenable. Although these features are well suited to making capital out

[9] Christopher Fry: *The Lady's Not for Burning* (London: Oxford University Press; 1949).

of contemporary world problems and individual anxieties, they were not deliberately invented for this purpose.

It would be surprising if the situation were otherwise. For one of the most important factors leading up to the twentieth-century crisis of Protestantism and the revolt against liberalism is just the fact that throughout most of its history Protestantism had been closely allied with the rationalist tradition. Although Luther, in a famous and typically earthy outburst, remarked that "reason is a whore," a *mésalliance* is an alliance for all that. Both Luther and his more fastidious disciple and colleague Melanchthon eagerly sought the aid of Renaissance humanism in order to justify and rationalize their own repudiation of Catholic authority.

In addition to the practical bonds provided by a common opposition to the intellectual and spiritual authority of Rome, Protestantism and rationalism also shared an optimistic theory of knowledge which seemed theoretically to justify that rejection. The Protestant view that the Bible, the Word of God, was an open book which men, once they had cast off the shackles of tradition, could read and understand without the mediative interpretation of an authority, echoed in religious form the epistemology of the new science, which regarded Nature as an open book, directly accessible to man—either through his senses, as in Bacon's philosophy, or through his intellect, as in the methodology of Descartes—independently of the interpretation of the Church. As the *veracitas dei* made manifest the religious truth of The Book, when approached in the proper spirit, so the *veracitas naturae* made manifest the scientific truth of the Book of Nature when approached in the proper spirit.[1] The optimistic anti-authoritarian view that man was able to apprehend the truth by his own efforts was influential both in the birth of Protestantism and in the rebirth of rationalism in the sixteenth century.

For this reason alone, none of the notorious clashes between science and religion—neither Luther's rejection of the ideas of "the fool" Copernicus, who "wants to turn the whole art of astronomy upside down" in defiance of the book of Joshua,[2] nor John Wesley's pronouncement, as late as 1768, that "the giving up of witchcraft is in effect the giving up of the Bible" [3]—should be allowed to obscure the fact that during most of Protestantism's short history, its intellectual leaders, with a few exceptions, have taken for granted that the results of autonomous intellectual inquiry would be in ultimate harmony—whatever difficulties might turn up along the way—with Protestant religious thought.[4] The New England lightning-rod controversy of 1755 is a more representative case than those already cited. The Reverend Thomas Prince delivered a sermon at Boston's Old South Church in which he ascribed the frequency of earthquakes that year to the erection of "iron points invented by the sagacious Mr. Franklin." "In Boston," he pointed out, "are more erected than anywhere else in New

[1] For the idea of the optimistic epistemology of manifest truth, see Popper: "On the Sources . . . ," op. cit. See also Barth: *From Rousseau to Ritschl* (London: SCM Press Ltd.; 1959), p. 53.

[2] See Luther: *Tischreden* (Weimar: Hermann Böhlaus; 1916), Vol. IV, p. 4638.

[3] Andrew D. White: *The Warfare of Science and Theology* (London: Macmillan & Co.; 1896), I, p. 363.

[4] James Luther Adams: "Tillich's Concept of the Protestant Era," printed in Paul Tillich: *The Protestant Era* (Chicago: Chicago University Press; 1948), pp. 277 ff.

England, and Boston seems to be more dreadfully shaken. Oh! there is no getting out of the mighty hand of God." [5] Professor John Winthrop, a Harvard theologian, promptly replied that it could hardly be impious to prevent thunder and lightning—both tokens of divine displeasure—from doing their proper work. "It is as much our duty to secure ourselves against the effects of lightning," Winthrop explained, "as against those of rain, snow, and wind by the means God has put into our hands." [6]

It is only in the present century that the assumption of harmony between reason and Protestant thought has really broken down and the relationship been severed both in theory and in practice. Now, not in Luther's time, the whore is symbolical of Protestantism's relationship to reason. Now reason is something to be indulged in from time to time with no sense of responsibility; previously it was a partner in a very stormy marriage. And this is the main cause of the present crisis of identity in Protestantism. Yet even here the retreat into irrationalism has been motivated by rational considerations, not simply by some irrational "spirit of the age." Moreover, the new Protestants believe they have a rational excuse, through the "problem of ultimate commitment," for an irrational commitment to their "independent standing ground."

These reservations about the common interpretation of the background of contemporary Protestant thought as an irrationalist development themselves need to be examined carefully. That a way of thinking can be considered a rea-

[5] A. D. White: *Warfare*, I, p. 366.
[6] Ibid., p. 366.

sonable, fairly logical development does not in itself make
that thought acceptable: a logical development does not
necessarily lead to true conclusions unless its premises are
also true. And many of the premises of contemporary theology are false, as I shall attempt to show later. In addition,
that the movement away from liberalism was sound does
not mean that most people who participated, even most of
the leaders, necessarily did so for sound reasons. Almost any
widespread intellectual shift involves many different moti-
vations. Some people move with the crowd; some simply
take a fancy to a theory they do not understand at all; others revolt for "reasons" which are too irrational to describe.
Finally, the fact that a shift in intellectual perspective has
been carried out deliberately and logically, rather than arising from deep-seated passion, does not, even from a rationalist point of view, make it necessarily more admirable.
Indeed, one of the least attractive features of the new Protestantism is the Machiavellian coldness and calculation with
which it has been championed as the best means to insure
the survival of institutional Protestantism. This mood appears even in Karl Barth (see chapter III, section 2), whose
earliest published complaint about Protestant liberalism
was that it did not give him strong enough material for his
sermons.[7] And it is echoed in the rather tiresome spirit of
annoyance—the "we must stop letting ourselves be pushed
around" attitude—which is suggested in Fosdick's sermon
and which echoes throughout the new thinking. What is
usually lacking in the new Protestantism's reasonable retreat from reason is just that passionate depth which makes

[7] Barth: "Moderne Theologie und Reichgottesarbeit," *Zeitschrift für
Theologie und Kirche*, 1909, pp. 317–21.

certain other twentieth-century revolts against reason relatively attractive: for example, the rebellion against reason
(involving an erroneous notion of reason) in the name of
fundamental human relationships which Koestler recorded
in *Darkness at Noon,* or the protest against the so-called scientific spirit of Marxism which Pasternak tried to live out in
his oppressive society.[8]

Nevertheless, I shall emphasize the considerations behind the shift which seem to me to be the most rational,
in an effort to be as fair as possible to a position I fundamentally oppose. The account I am about to give is intended, first, as a partial reconstruction of the problem
situation that thinking Protestants faced and to a large extent continue to face. Second, and more important, this
analysis will serve as background for the philosophical problems I shall discuss.

3 · *The Rise of Protestant Liberalism*

Problems of Christian identity are not new to Protestantism or to modern times. The seeds of what is sometimes
described as the search for the substance or essence of Christianity were perhaps sown by Jesus himself, in his secre-
tiveness about his belief that he was the Messiah. However
this may be, the requirements of Christian faith and practice, as distinct from the question of Jesus' own identity,
were already an important issue during the early life of the
church. This can be seen from a record in the Book of
Acts (chapter 15) of an early debate among the disciples in

---

[8] See John Strachey: "The Strangled Cry," *Encounter,* November and
December 1960; and Reinhold Niebuhr: "Strachey's Cry," *Encounter,*
January 1961.

Jerusalem. St. Paul, St. Peter, and St. James, among "great dissension," gathered to debate whether obedience to the laws of Moses, including the requirement of circumcision, was essential to Christian practice. Circumcision, they eventually decided, was nonessential; and early Christianity, profiting from the decision, spread among the Gentiles less painfully. In a perhaps perverted sense, this particular issue is still alive. In 1958 Reinhold Niebuhr argued that it is no longer essential for Christians to carry on evangelistic activity among the Jews.[9] The apostles in Jerusalem, who had in effect been debating whether Christian evangelism could rightly be carried on anywhere else, might have been surprised at Niebuhr's view.

In the nearly two thousand years of Christianity between St. Paul and Reinhold Niebuhr, there have been repeated controversies about the fundaments of Christianity—its cosmology, its philosophy, its claims about the scriptures, its ethics. The essentiality of each of these has been debated in turn. Indeed, from one point of view it might be said that issues of self-identity have provided the main intellectual problems of Christianity throughout its history.

Such problems have been most acute in the various Protestant branches of Christianity, which by their very structure and by their intellectual and political alliances and attitudes have been highly susceptible to erosion. To the extent that it is just another form of the debate about Christian identity, the new Protestant thought might be regarded as but the latest manifestation of concern about these

[9] See Reinhold Niebuhr: *Pious and Secular America* (New York: Charles Scribner's Sons; 1958); and my review of it in *Commentary*, March 1959.

problems. Even so, the debate enters an entirely new plane with the appearance of the new thought. For the new Protestant thought is far less a response to disagreement about Christian identity than a response to a gnawing fear among Protestants of total loss of Christian identity.

Since this fear arose from the collapse of Protestant liberalism, it will be necessary to review this point of view briefly in order to put the new Protestant thought in context. Here it was that the search for identity in Christianity came to a climax; here the explosive force latent in the very presuppositions of such a search was finally ignited.

An eminent Protestant liberal, Theodore T. Munger, wrote in 1883: "If Christianity has any human basis, it is its entire reasonableness. It must not only sit easily on the mind, but it must ally itself with it in all its normal action." [1] This is a characteristic liberal utterance—not only in its conviction of the reasonableness of Christianity but in its assumption that Christianity has a "human basis." During the nineteenth century, certain philosophical, psychological, moral, and political assumptions—all of them reasonable within the context of nineteenth-century thought —so meshed with an equally reasonable interpretation of the message of the historical Jesus that liberal Protestantism, the fusion of those assumptions and that interpretation, seemed the most radically reasonable religious position. In this period it was not only possible but easy for a man, without tension or duplicity, to identify with both Protestant Christian and rationalist traditions, to be both Christo-centric and rationalist, both Christian and "modern

[1] See Herbert W. Schneider: *Religion in 20th Century America* (Cambridge: Harvard University Press; 1952), p. 119.

man." If such a man could serve two masters, it was because those masters were partners.

There have been two main varieties of Protestant liberalism in America, and Munger spoke as a member of the
later type. The earlier Protestant liberalism was itself divided, comprising both Jeffersonian Deism and the rather
more conservative Unitarianism of the late eighteenth century. Both of these had resulted in part from opposition to
the Calvinist doctrines of human depravity and divine
election. And many of their intellectual leaders agreed in
accepting the philosophical psychology of John Locke and
in adhering—here also supported by Locke—to the eighteenth century's "natural religion," with its first-cause and
design arguments for the existence of God, and its many
other "proofs" and evidences for the main principles of religion.

Although most contemporary theologians are quite opposed to the earlier variety, it is the later style that they
have usually had in mind in their polemics against Protestant liberalism. Such attacks are generally directed at the influential turn-of-the-century liberal systems of such men as
Walter Rauschenbusch and Shailer Mathews in America,
and Albrecht Ritschl and Adolf von Harnack in Germany.
These later liberal systems sprang from an emphatic *rejection* of the Lockean tenets that had undergirded the earlier
liberalism, and from a rather enthusiastic acceptance of the
leading themes of Kantian and post-Kantian German
"idealism."

This type of liberalism first appeared in America early
in the nineteenth century in the New England transcendentalist movement, a tiny "greater Boston" clique that suc-

cessfully overthrew the early Lockean liberalism within the Unitarian Church. Although New England transcendentalism never became a national church movement, as did subsequent forms of this variety of Protestant liberalism, its members were probably more articulate than their successors. Perry Miller has judged it "the most energetic and extensive upsurge of the mind and spirit enacted in America until the intellectual crisis of the 1920's." [2]

The transcendentalist movement began in the middle 1820's, when some of the most talented of Boston's Unitarian young people began to feel that they, like Achilles in Zeno's story, were taking an infinitely long time to reach their goal, an earthly New Jerusalem. They began to wonder aloud whether Americans were not being held back by their own Unitarian Church, and to complain about the materialism, complacency, and "low commercial tone" of their prosperous native Boston, and about the lack of any real enthusiasm, fervor, or spiritual quality—ingredients they thought necessary to keep spiritual life progressing in pace with material conditions. Their churches they accused of offering only a "religion of pale negations," something "satisfactory to Boston merchants and Harvard professors, but not to those who still cherished the ancient fire of Puritan mysticism or sought to realize the New World

---

[2] Perry Miller, ed.: *The Transcendentalists* (Cambridge: Harvard University Press; 1950), pp. 14 ff. For material relating to the transcendentalist movement, see also G. H. Williams, ed.: *The Harvard Divinity School* (Boston: Beacon Press; 1954); George F. Whicher, ed.: *The Transcendentalist Revolt against Materialism* (Boston: D. C. Heath and Company; 1949); and Octavius Brooks Frothingham: *Transcendentalism in New England* (New York: Harper & Brothers; 1959). Miller's excellent anthology is especially valuable for a study of the religious aspects of the movement.

dream of a regenerate humanity." [3] "Corpse-cold," concluded Emerson. "The heart is pulverized," echoed Ripley.
Dissatisfied spiritually, the young transcendentalists sought
to effect a "change of heart" among their compatriots.

They found a philosophy to nurse their dissatisfactions
and spur their hopes in the pages of the new European periodicals that their Unitarian fathers and relatives had or-
dered for the Boston Athenaeum in order to keep in touch
with the European Enlightenment. Although the light
across the Atlantic had not been extinguished, Europe had
been having an intellectual revolution of its own while the
Unitarians were quarreling with the Calvinists. Locke's philosophy was now widely and authoritatively considered,
among European thinkers, to have been refuted by the work
of Hume and Kant. After reading the accounts of this revolution in European thought—first in the English writings
of Carlyle, Coleridge, and Wordsworth, and later in the
original German of thinkers such as Kant, Schleiermacher,
and Strauss—the young Unitarians drew their conclusions.
If Unitarianism as they knew it rested on Locke's philosophical psychology, and if this had been refuted, Unitarianism was intellectually bankrupt. That it was spiritually
bankrupt they were already convinced. Moreover, the new
German philosophy seemed to provide just that enthusiasm, depth, and moral fervor—in addition to the call for a
"change of heart"—which was needed to effect a revolution in human motivation to match the revolution in man's
material condition which the American republic had already begun to achieve.

The transcendentalists later came into direct and often

[3] Whicher: Introduction to *The Transcendentalist Revolt*, p. vi.

personal touch with the new continental thinking. In March 1836, for example, Ripley published in the *Christian Examiner* a study and defense of Schleiermacher's theology, recommending it as a possible ground of synthesis and reconciliation between the still-warring factions of Calvinism and Lockean Unitarianism.[4] In May 1841 Theodore Parker delivered his famous "Discourse of the Transient and Permanent in Christianity"—following by only two years the essay of the German theologian and historian David Strauss, *Vergängliches und Bleibendes in Christentum* (The Transient and the Permanent in Christianity).[5] "Christianity," Parker announced, "is a simple thing, very simple. It is absolute, pure morality. . . . All this is very simple—a little child can understand it. . . ."[6]

Despite considerable initial opposition, the transcendentalists eventually won an effective victory within Unitarianism. Yet the entry of transcendentalist thought into the mainstream of American Protestantism, traditionally suspicious of anything smacking of Unitarianism, was to be delayed until the closing years of the nineteenth century, when, having been baptized by the efforts of Horace Bushnell, it was popularly christened "Protestant liberalism." Not until 1907 did the Baptist theologian Rauschenbusch, now regarded as one of Protestant liberalism's more repre-

---

[4] George Ripley: "Schleiermacher as a Theologian," *The Christian Examiner*, XX, pp. 1–46; reprinted in Miller's anthology, pp. 99–102.

[5] Parker's discourse is reprinted in Miller's anthology, pp. 259–83. Parker acknowledges his indebtedness to Strauss's historical work in his farewell letter to his congregation, "Theodore Parker's Experience as a Minister," excerpts of which are reprinted in Miller, pp. 484–93.

[6] Miller: op. cit., p. 277.

sentative American exponents, expound such views in his influential *Christianity and the Social Crisis*. Even then, it was another decade before the movement gained any really important following among the clergy.

Why, despite its early appearance in Boston, was Protestant liberalism denied a wide hearing for so long? Although a sharp attack by Calvinist thinkers certainly helped weaken its impact, most historians blame the "theological lassitude" that pervaded most American religious thought from the end of the eighteenth century until the last quarter of the nineteenth.[7] In those last and very revolutionary twenty-five years, however, Darwin's theories, the dramatic new evolutionary philosophies which provided easy-to-understand challenges to the story of creation as given in Genesis, combined with latent disgust at the excesses of Calvinist evangelistic revivalism, finally forced the theologians to reconsider their assumptions. The industrial revolution forced them to review their social and ethical ideas as well; until the closing quarter of the nineteenth century, Protestant thought had usually patronized the social *status quo*.

Yet, even if Protestantism was now severely challenged both intellectually and socially, evolutionary theory and the industrial revolution were not by themselves sufficient to push it into liberalism. It was easy enough for a theologian to combine evolutionary views with Andrew Carnegie's Gospel of Wealth: "wealthy man equals fit man equals good man equals Christian man." In this equation God

[7] See Sidney E. Mead: "American Protestantism Since the Civil War, II," *Journal of Religion*, April 1956, p. 75: "Since the end of the 18th century, the bulk of the Protestant denominations had cultivated scholastic orthodoxy, enlivened and more or less sentimentalized by pietistic revivalism and apart from the spirit and mind of modern civilization."

helps those who help themselves by living a hard-working Protestant Christian life, and heaps rewards upon them in this life. Poverty, said the great Civil War preacher Henry Ward Beecher, is the consequence of sin, even though he was later to show in his own personal life that one can sin without being impoverished. Christ's ethic became the practice of the "all-round-American boy" and the successful businessman. The late Episcopal Bishop William Lawrence of Massachusetts, a very rich man, even suggested that one's wealth was an index to one's godliness. "Godliness is in league with riches," he affirmed. "In the long run, it is only to the man of morality that wealth comes." [8] Christ, for many people, became a sort of bearded Dale Carnegie who did not charge for lessons.

Yet, although some thinkers could combine the evolutionist threat with a reaffirmation of Calvinist belief and Protestant identification with the social *status quo*, many others—though equally "evolutionist"—could not. The suffering and injustices resulting from industrialization were too blatant to be overlooked or explained away. Whatever might happen in the long run, in the visible short run any God who helped the robber barons seemed indeed to be helping those who helped themselves . . . to other people's money. Earlier transcendentalism had evolved as a literary and philosophical movement, struck less by social injustice than by social "lack of depth," and had later added a social program to its program of "motivational" reform. Protestant liberalism now arose in response to urgent so-

[8] Reprinted in *Democracy and the Gospel of Wealth*, ed. by Gail Kennedy (Boston: D. C. Heath and Company; 1949), p. 69. Lawrence's address, "The Relation of Wealth to Morals," first appeared in the *World's Work*, January 1901.

cial problems and seized on the already developed trans-cendentalist philosophy as a useful instrument to justify its social program. In it the social reformers found the two things they most needed: a basis for their social program, and an effective way to reconcile science and religion. The considered viewpoint resulting from this pragmatic wedding between Protestant social reformers and transcendentalist philosophy is what contemporary theologians usually have in mind when they speak of Protestant liberalism.

Perhaps this viewpoint can be best understood by re-viewing some of the most important Protestant liberal be-liefs about ethics, politics, and the historical Jesus.

4 · The Liberal Understanding of Jesus

For most liberal Protestants, the historical Jesus was their strong ally in the battle against Calvinist orthodoxy and social injustice, and their great general in the fight for a regeneration of culture.

He was a strong ally because the Calvinists had assumed that the Christ of Christian dogma—the Jesus who had, at least since the early Chalcedon decision, been emphasized in the theological writings of the church—was the same as the Jesus of history. What better way to scatter the forces of Calvinism than to refute such assumptions by bring-ing back the Jesus of history to mock such misinterpreta-tions of his message? If it could be shown through histori-cal research that the historical Jesus had taught a message vastly different from that ascribed by the Calvinists to the Christ of dogma, the very core of Calvinism would be de-stroyed. Hence the liberal Protestants, first in Germany and later in America, enthusiastically undertook research in

Biblical criticism and began the famous quest for the historical Jesus. Jesus was also the great general of the liberal Protestants. Their leader, teacher, and guide in the fight for personal and social transformation, he had, they thought, given men the key for cultural reform in the guise of the most spiritual ethic the world had ever known. The crux of his message, they agreed, was the call for a *metanoia*, a conversion, repentance, or radical change of attitude toward life.[9]

Throughout their investigations, the liberals sought to give this picture of the historical Christ a firm historical basis by means of scriptural study and independent research into the history of Jesus' time. At first, one of their more powerful aids was the belief that the gospel of St. John presented the oldest and most accurate narrative of Christ's teaching and life, probably even the report of an eyewitness. It was in this Fourth Gospel that the idea of change of attitude was emphasized, here that the idea of the Kingdom of God on earth and the picture of Jesus as a great spiritual teacher were least ambiguous. The first three Synoptic Gospels, on the other hand, in view of their many descriptions of miracles and claims about a supermundane kingdom, could be regarded as rather primitive distortions of Jesus' message on which the church had mistakenly fastened.[1] Under the penetrating searchlight of the liberals,

[9] For a beautifully stated example of the "change-of-attitude" interpretation of Christ's message, see Vladimir G. Simkhovitch: *Toward the Understanding of Jesus* (New York: The Macmillan Company; 1921).

[1] "I take it as established that the Gospel of John is the narrative of an eyewitness and forms an organic whole," wrote Schleiermacher. Quoted by Albert Schweitzer in *The Quest of the Historical Jesus* (London: A. & C. Black; 1910) p. 66.

the historical Jesus, long buried under misinterpretations and false dogma, seemed to come to life after centuries of misunderstanding, and eagerly to endorse and bless the liberals' own ideas.

This obliging agreement enabled the liberal Protestants to remain sincere Christians. On the one hand, many features of the modernity they had embraced seemed to lead away from Christianity: they were forced to reject its ancient metaphysics, its estimate of man, its authoritarian temper. But at the critical moment, when they otherwise would have had in sincerity to abandon Christianity, the latest results of their historical investigations presented them with a picture of Jesus to which they could assent after all. If they could in fact accept the message and person of the true Jesus of history, they had a right—indeed a stronger right than the Calvinists—to call themselves Christians.

That the message of a great religious teacher should be an ethical one accorded with the Kantian and post-Kantian belief that ethics is the core of religion—a significant agreement, considering the influence Kant's thought exerted on the liberals. Jesus now appeared as the greatest of religious teachers because the liberals found that he had lived in perfect accordance with whatever "facts of human consciousness" they thought basic to the moral life—whether *duty*, as in Kant, or "absolute dependence," as in Schleiermacher. To follow Jesus' example, they argued, would be to transform one's own life and to contribute to the ultimate transformation of cultural existence.

5 · *Political and Psychological Assumptions of Protestant Liberalism*

Whereas liberal Biblical scholarship indicated that Jesus *intended* his ethic as a practical social gospel, and that his ethical remarks had formed the core of his teaching, the chief politico-psychological assumption of Protestant liberalism was that Jesus' ethic was in fact practical.

The Protestant liberals considered a *revolution in human motivation* to be the chief political need of their time. This was Kant's suggestion in *Religion Within the Limits of Reason Alone;* and it was Rauschenbusch's conception in 1907. Even as late as 1933 the Federal Council of Churches proclaimed that "the Christian conscience can be satisfied with nothing less than the complete substitution of motives of mutual helpfulness and good will for the motive of private gain." [2]

The principal reason for the fact that the liberals centered their hopes on a change in human motivation is not difficult to find. As they analysed the social order of their day, they concluded that many economic and social institutions worked against social justice. Yet, strongly influenced by Marxist analysis, they believed there was little hope of reforming these institutions from within, since the institutions themselves encouraged greed and selfishness and an economic individualism that was opposed in spirit to the imposition of the social controls the liberals thought were necessary. The social circle was a vicious one: the institutions encouraged wrong attitudes, and the wrong attitudes helped perpetuate unjust institutions. Since most liberal

[2] See Schneider: op. cit., p. 77.

Protestants were, unlike Marx, opposed in principle to a
violent social revolution aimed at changing social and
economic institutions by force, they were compelled to focus their efforts on the task of changing human attitudes.
Such an effort to revolutionize men's attitudes seemed to
them a *Christian* program, since they believed that the
change of motivation which was required would have to involve a shift from the profit motive to the selfless, "mutual
service" motivation they considered part of the ethic of the
Sermon on the Mount.

The vague liberal assumptions about man's "dignity,"
and their Kantian belief that the obligation to do one's
duty was a universal human experience, led many of them
to feel that such a change of attitude was possible on a large
scale. Few of them were definite about just what kind of
social institutions would accompany that change. But they
agreed that in principle a set of practical social and economic institutions existed which would be compatible with
the ethic of the Sermon. Human motivation and social justice could, in principle, be reconciled, however they might
cancel each other out at the moment.

If the only solution to social problems lay in a widespread
revolution in motivation, and if the Christian churches
were the custodians of the only ethic based on the proper
motivation, then the Christian churches had an all-important role in the social order. On them, literally, lay the task
not only of regenerating society and eventually bringing in
the Kingdom of God but of saving society from chaos and
violent revolution. To some of the more liberal liberals, this
was not only the present duty of Christians; the establishment of the Kingdom of God on earth was the ultimate goal

of Christianity. The resulting feeling of ominous responsibility in the face of social crisis lent some excitement and fervor to the program.

The notion that it was feasible for the churchmen of America to effect a world-wide revolution in human motivation would probably have been impossible without a widespread *popular* belief that progress, however it might be delayed, was *inevitable*. The theology of progress—fostered in America by the Enlightenment philosophy, encouraged by long periods of peace and by relative economic progress, and endorsed by evolutionary theory—allowed the ordinary liberal Protestant to embrace a utopianism that would have shocked the most optimistic Jeffersonian and the wildest dreamer among the political *philosophes* of the eighteenth century.

An optimism that seems unbelievable today was not, however, the unique property of the Protestant liberals; it underlay a surprisingly large part of late nineteenth-century culture. Even an acute observer like George Santayana was able to write in his essay "The Intellectual Temper of the Age," published just before World War I:

> Our bodies in this generation are generally safe, and often comfortable; and for those who can suspend their irrational labours long enough to look about them, the spectacle of the world, if not particularly beautiful or touching, presents a rapid and crowded drama and (what here concerns me most) one usually intelligible. . . . We are not condemned, as most generations have been, to fight and believe without an inkling of

the cause. . . . The whole drift of things presents a
huge, good-natured comedy to the observer. It stirs not
unpleasantly a certain sturdy animality and hearty self-
trust which lie at the base of human nature.[3]

On a somewhat less sophisticated level—that of Edward
Bellamy's famous prophecy, Looking Backward—a preacher
in the year 2000 looks backward to the year 1887, forward
to the future, and concludes his Sunday sermon with these
words:

With a tear for the dark past, turn we then to the daz-
zling future, and, veiling our eyes, press forward. The
long and weary winter of the race is ended. Its summer
has begun. Humanity has burst the chrysalis. The heav-
ens are before it.[4]

At least the advice to veil our eyes was sound.

6 · The Decline of Protestant Liberalism

> "You forget," said the Devil with a chuckle,
> "that I have been evolving too."
>
> W. R. INGE

Thirteen years after the publication of the passage I have
just quoted, Santayana prepared a new introduction for his
Winds of Doctrine. He no longer felt so safe—not even
about "our bodies in this generation." "That comfortable
liberal world," he now wrote, "was like a great tree with the
trunk already sawed quite through, but still standing with

[3] Winds of Doctrine, pp. 2–3.
[4] Edward Bellamy: Looking Backward: 2000–1887 (London: Alvin
Redman, Ltd.; 1948), p. 208. First published in 1888.

all its leaves quietly rustling, and with us dozing under its shade. We were inexpressibly surprised when it fell and half crushed us. . . ." [5]

Whereas the detached Santayana might be only inexpressibly surprised after a tree had half crushed him, many of his contemporaries blinked open their eyes with far less equanimity to an unshaded and not very brave new world. Their attempts to understand what had happened triggered the feverish intellectual activity that is familiarly characteristic in this period. The studies, as well as the dance halls, were roaring in the twenties.

Most of the events and ideas that occasioned the lapse of confidence in liberalism generally, not just in Protestant liberalism, made vivid, if not wholly accurate, impressions on this generation. Buttressing a dramatically colorful and imaginative theory with clinical detail, Freud helped shatter popularly man's high estimate of his own selflessness and rationality, his belief that he was at least master of his own belfry. World War I, the rise of the secular authoritarianisms, and the gradual failure of the League of Nations, all unintended developments, helped to topple the conceptions of personal and social progress and rational planning which had so comfortably undergirded liberalism and the Social Gospel. Though much naïve optimism survived World War I, within the United States if not elsewhere, the Depression muzzled even that. The popular tune of the 1920's, "My God, How the Money Rolls In," gave way, after 1929, to "Brother, Can You Spare a

[5] Santayana: Preface to the 1926 edition of *Winds of Doctrine* (New York: Charles Scribner's Sons), p. vi.

Dime?" and "Sing Me a Song of Social Significance." The promise of a chicken in every pot became a prayer for anything in the pot.

By World War II, which began with the whimper of the "phony war" and ended in the bang of Nagasaki, some men not only had begun to doubt human capacity to keep pace with science, and the "ultimate satisfactoriness" of scientific achievement, but even wondered whether the rise of science itself was not a cloud upon the future. The pietistic fall-out of the nineteenth century gave way to a more menacing sort of rain; faith in the future was replaced by adulation of the passing moment. "Enjoy Yourself, It's Later Than You Think" now hit the Hit Parade. The struggle for the survival of the fittest was replaced by the struggle for the survival of anyone.

On a more abstract level, the philosophical assumptions of liberalism were also crumbling. Its post-Kantian idealism was heavily attacked by a new wave of empiricism which arose during World War I and the 1920's, led by the onslaught of pragmatism and the new logical positivism. Moreover, most of Kant's categories, which had been thought to be necessary mental principles, had by now broken down—shattering one of the last defenses of the notion that we could at least be certain about our innate prejudices and about the way in which our minds "imposed their nature" on reality. Kant thought that an alternative to Euclidean geometry was inconceivable. But the invention of non-Euclidean geometry showed that this was not so. Kant thought that we had to see the world of nature in terms of Newton's dynamics, and that an alternative was inconceivable. But Einstein's theory of relativity showed that this was not true either.[6]

How did these events and discoveries affect *Protestant liberalism* in particular? Any causal analysis of the historical situation would probably lead to the conclusion that this succession of social and intellectual explosions was principally responsible for the shift from optimistic Protestant liberalism to the pessimistic mood of neo-orthodoxy, the "theology of crisis." Here I am not primarily interested in an exact causal analysis but in the question whether the shift was intellectually justifiable. The answer must, I think, be affirmative.

Protestant liberalism could have survived most of these blows within the critical and rationalist tradition. The Bible, for example, contained rich material for a more tragic and realistic analysis of human existence and a deeper interpretation of human personality. It is hardly necessary, moreover, for a liberal to believe that men every day and in every way grow better and better. In fact, more sophisticated liberals such as Dewey, Shailer Mathews, and Ritschl did not feel as naïvely optimistic as is often stated: their progressivism was a *program* they were perhaps overly confident about, but rarely a *prediction*. Indeed, inevitable progress was itself a hang-over of the anthropomorphic theism they had already abandoned, a hang-over which looked at his-

[6] Kant also thought we must see nature in terms of the "law of causality," and that such a determinism was implied by Newtonian physics. More recently, Popper has argued that even classical physics—not to mention modern quantum physics—was indeterministic. See his "Indeterminism in Quantum Physics and in Classical Physics," *British Journal for the Philosophy of Science*, I (1950–51); and his forthcoming *Postscript to the Logic of Scientific Discovery*.

tory as a play with a steady build-up to a happy ending. Such considerations probably explain why one occasionally hears a neo-orthodox theologian claim, without any attempt to sound paradoxical, that his own viewpoint is at heart in the tradition of Protestant liberalism; that the Protestant liberals, stunned by the simultaneous collapse of so many of their assumptions, tended to cling to them desperately and *irrationally* and thereby to abandon *real* liberalism for the sake of an *arrested form* of liberalism, to identify the particular form and emphases of turn-of-the-century liberalism with the liberal spirit. There is a great deal of truth in such contentions. On a more fundamental level, however, the neo-orthodox claim to represent a more liberal Protestant liberalism is unjustified. The collapse of at least one assumption of Protestant liberalism could hardly have been survived within the liberal rationalist tradition. This was the Protestant liberal interpretation of the historical Jesus. Without this, a Protestant Christianity in the rationalist tradition became impossible; and hence a shift away from Protestant liberalism—and not only from a particular historical form of it—became intellectually imperative.

To clarify this very important point, we need to consider why the liberal interpretation of Jesus collapsed, and then to examine the formidable problems for Protestant liberalism which grew from the ruins.

7 · *The Liberal Jesus Vanishes*

The Protestant liberals inaugurated the historical criticism of the New Testament and the quest for the historical Jesus in the hope that the Nazarene might rise up as their

ally against the Calvinists and others who, they believed,
had dogmatically twisted his spiritual message into the call
to obedience before "mystery, miracle, and authority." The
early results of this criticism nourished this hope, increased
the plausibility of their program, and encouraged them to
continue.

Further research, however, revealed that the historical
Jesus was far more intractable than a good liberal might
have expected—particularly from another liberal. In so
far as the historical personality, Jesus of Nazareth, could be
restored to life at all, it tended to haunt the liberals and to
bless, even if reservedly, the Calvinists it had been expected
to disown. By 1910 Francis Crawford Burkitt, introducing
the first English translation of Albert Schweitzer's *The
Quest of the Historical Jesus*, solemnly rebuked the liberals
with these words:

. . . when the alternative of "Jesus or Christ" is put
forward, as it has been in a recent publication, or when
we are bidden to choose between the Jesus of history
and the Christ of dogma, few except professed students
know what a protean and kaleidoscopic figure the "Jesus of history" is . . . we are beginning to see that the
apocalyptic vision, the New Age which God is to bring
in, is no mere embroidery of Christianity, but the heart
of its enthusiasm. And therefore the expectation of vindication and judgment to come, the imagery of the Mes-
sianic Feast, the "other-worldiness" against which so
many eloquent words were said in the nineteenth century, are not to be regarded as regrettable accretions
foisted on by superstition to the pure morality of the

original Gospel. These ideas are the Christian Hope
. . . not to be given up so long as we remain Christians at all.[7]

What had happened, when described in detail, makes a
complex and exciting story. Basically, however, the result
was fairly simple: so many problems arose out of the attempt to find a liberal Jesus in the historical documents
that eventually the entire program collapsed from within.
The central historical problem which proved the undoing
of the liberals concerned the eschatological content of
Christ's message, that is, his view of the nature of the coming Kingdom of God. Did the historical Jesus build on the
presuppositions of late Jewish eschatology concerning the
coming of the Messiah and the supernatural Kingdom of
God? Or did he build on a foundation that preached an
ethic of love simply for the purpose of regenerating the culture of *this* world? The three Synoptic Gospels, Matthew,
Mark, and Luke, seemed to support the first view; the best
props for the latter view were to be found in the gospel of
St. John. At first, attempts were made to reconcile the two
interpretations, to co-ordinate the Christ of the Synoptic
Gospels and Jewish eschatology with the Jesus who was
thought to have preached that his Messiahship and the
heavenly kingdom were purely spiritual. All attempts at
reconciliation, however, broke down: it had to be one or the
other.[8]

Eventually, through the work of such historians as Jo-
hannes Weiss and Schweitzer, the first view triumphed. The

[7] F. C. Burkitt, in his Preface to Schweitzer: *The Quest.*
[8] Schweitzer: Introduction to the third edition of *The Quest,* 1954.

Pauline epistles and Mark's gospel became accepted as the earliest and most reliable historical documents; the gospel of John was now regarded as a later literary and philosophical reinterpretation of Jesus' life, written for the apologetic purpose of explaining why Christ and the Kingdom of God had failed to come. It introduced the idea of a *spiritual Kingdom* within men and spiritualized the message and portrait of Jesus. In his great book by that name, Schweitzer magnificently chronicled and made generally available the results of this "quest of the historical Jesus," which lasted for four generations during the nineteenth century and commanded the efforts and attention of some of the most powerful minds in German historical scholarship.

After Schweitzer's report, it was no longer possible to claim that the historical Jesus was faithfully portrayed by the persuasive liberal picture of the moral teacher, the surpassingly good man who taught the fatherhood of God and the brotherhood of man without making any supernatural claims. The real Jesus, as far as the most advanced branch of historical research into Biblical foundations could tell, had preached an early supernatural return; his ideas had been thoroughly conditioned by the Jewish eschatology of his time. Later independent historical investigations into Jewish eschatological views corroborated these conclusions. From now on, anyone who was to be faithful to the historical Jesus would have to take into account that he was apparently convinced of his eschatological message and his divine mission. His purpose, as he had apparently conceived it, was to establish the Kingdom of God on the side of God and in tension with, if not simply against, the kingdom of this world. The message he preached was not intended as an ethical key for the transformation of the worldly kingdom. He was not a leader and teacher of culture, but an opponent of culture who *threatened* mankind with his promise to come to judge those who identified themselves with the hopes of this world's culture. Schweitzer writes:

> The spiritual life of our own time seems like to perish at His hands, for He leads to battle against our thought a host of dead ideas, a ghostly army upon which death has no power, and Himself destroys again the truth and goodness which His Spirit creates in us, so that it cannot rule the world.

In short, the liberal picture of Jesus had apparently been unhistorical.

This new view of the historical Jesus also forced the liberals to entertain seriously an uncongenial view of the Christian Church. Partly because of a certain anticlericalism among some of the socialist movements that had aligned themselves with Protestant liberalism, partly for their own reasons, the liberals had been fond of emphasizing the *individual* Christian and minimizing the role of the organized church in Christianity. Jesus himself, they argued, had not intended to found a church; the church was a later development, formed under pressure.

The eschatological theme, however, now brought into focus the New Testament emphasis on the role of the church, or community of believers; showed how important such a group would be for the fulfillment of Jesus' eschatological claims and expectations; and related it, further, to the famous Old Testament idea of the "remnant" of the faithful whence redemption would come to mankind. This re-evaluation of the role and Biblical basis of the church helped strengthen the already growing call for ecumenical unity among Protestant groups.

If the New Testament's apparent endorsement of the idea of an organized church was unwelcome to some liberals, the implications for the Christian ethic which the new understanding of the historical Jesus involved were far more disagreeable. The Sermon on the Mount, it appeared, had never been intended by Jesus as a practical ethic for this world. To use Schweitzer's phrase, Jesus had advocated a temporary *interims Ethik* for the use of his followers—who mistakenly expected, as did Jesus himself, that the coming of a *supernatural* Kingdom of God would quickly follow his crucifixion. If the supernatural Kingdom of God was about to come, those who expected to enter it hardly needed an applicable ethic in terms of *this* world's needs; the most prudent move for men holding such expectations was in fact the abandonment of the goods and attachments of this world, as indicated in the Sermon, in preparation for the expected spiritual apotheosis of the next.

However, since Jesus and his followers had been mistaken, and since there was no way of predicting when, if ever, the heavenly kingdom would arrive, any ethic founded on an expectation of its immediate advent could not be expected to be politically or personally practical as a guide for the establishment of a spiritualized kingdom of this world.

Of course, the fact that Jesus did not intend his ethic to be practical would not, by itself, exclude the possibility that the ethic might in fact be practical. He might have moralized more practically than he knew. However, the events of the twentieth century were illustrating dramatically that it was not in fact practical. The Protestant liberals had sought a change of attitude that would permit the ethic of the Sermon to be implemented in everyday political and economic experience, but Freud's observations about man's good will and rational capabilities made the possibility of such a widespread motivational transformation appear intellectually absurd. Liberalism was the bull in a bear market. As people began to realize, through trial and sometimes devastating error, that the direct application of such utopian ideas to practical politics could be foolish and self-defeating, liberalism also came to seem like the bull in the china shop.

The old utopianism—under which the slogan that World War I was a "war to end wars" or "to keep the world safe for democracy" was taken seriously enough to bring the churches to the support of the military program—was enervated by the war's far from utopian or democratic outcome. When some of the more callow assessments of the war began to appear, the sting of insult aggravated the hurt of failure. Once the war was over, the famous dean of London's St. Paul's Cathedral mocked the idealists. "During the war," Dean Inge wrote, "we said we were fighting to make the world safe for democracy. That was a lump of sugar for the American eagle, and fortunately for us, he swallowed it." [9] Hoover's pacifism, the studied attempts of America and the United Kingdom to pare down each other's navies during the 1930's while Hitler was marching to power, and the many other desperate, sometimes touch-

[9] William Ralph Inge, in *Living Philosophies* (New York: Simon and Schuster; 1931), pp. 307–17.

ing attempts to set things right all at once, contributed
further to the coming bitter harvest of foolhardy utopianism. The ethic of the Sermon on the Mount was indeed
impractical.

So the Protestant liberals, who had assumed that the
Christian religion, even divested of its cosmological content, would preserve an important social message, and who
had often retained their affiliation with Protestantism for
the sake of this social program, now learned that no social
ethic had been at the core of Jesus' message, and that even
if one had been, the particular ethic ascribed to him was
socially impractical. The obvious question could not help
arising: For what purpose should those who were primarily
interested in transforming culture continue their identification with Protestantism—particularly if they could not accept the ideas that appeared to be in fact at the basis of the
Christian message? As Burkitt had written: "These ideas
are the Christian hope . . . not to be given up so long as
we remain Christians at all."

8 · *Were the Liberals to Blame for the Liberal Picture of Jesus?*

The importance of these historical findings and the questions they engendered in confounding Protestant liberalism
can hardly be overestimated. Yet some critics of liberalism
have evoked an even more sweeping criticism of the liberals.
Not only were their facts wrong: their historical method
was radically incorrect, if not sinfully perverse. The liberals,
it is suggested, used Christ's person as a peg on which to
hang their prejudices and hopes. The resulting clothes-
horse personality they used as a persuasive social tool to

implement their dreams and to lend both rational plausibility and divine authority to their very human message.

This methodological complaint is basically just, but it
needs to be applied with some restraint. If the liberals are
guilty, they can hardly be blamed for it. They were, after all,
unaware of the complexity of Biblical research; and they
themselves were largely responsible for inaugurating and
continuing it, even after they had become conscious that
they were conspiring in their own undoing. Schweitzer is
too hard on them, even when he colors his severity with
ambiguity. After praising the relentless honesty of the liberals, he goes on elsewhere to castigate them vigorously for
not seeing the New Testament terrain as clearly as he himself had done. Twentieth-century New Testament historians like Schweitzer possess a sounder, more self-conscious
methodology largely because they have been able to build
on the liberals' far from deliberate or obvious methodological errors.[1] The man who invented the electric light did not
criticize the inventor of the candle.

The liberals gave to Jesus the kind of reverential yet unsatisfactory homage men have always paid to great person-
alities, great art, great literature—those phenomena, themselves ambiguous, which command the fealty of so many

---

[1] Although I believe this practice was usually carried out unconsciously,
there are occasional indications of a self-conscious awareness that the
historical Jesus was being made a peg for modern ethical ideals. For example, in Samuel Butler's *Erewhon Revisited*, the Sunchild has some
things to say which are explicitly intended to refer to developments in the
Anglican theology of the nineteenth century. The Sunchild, having returned to Erewhon, urges his followers to use his figure unabashedly for
their best ethical conceptions, so that "you will make me out to be much
better and abler than I was, or ever shall be. . . ." (London: Jonathan
Cape; 1927), p. 267.

different people for so many different reasons. Most men
like to think that anything of high repute contains at least
a fragment of themselves; it is hard to worship something
totally alien. "Critics who write about Shakespeare," according to W. H. Auden, "reveal more about themselves
than about Shakespeare, but perhaps that is the great value
of drama of the Shakespearean kind, namely, that whatever
he may see taking place on stage, its final effect upon each
spectator is a self-revelation." [2] Plato has repeatedly undergone the same treatment, as Werner Jaeger and others have
pointed out. One example Jaeger gives, the interpretation
of Plato presented by Schleiermacher, is interesting in itself, since Schleiermacher was also the first liberal theologian to begin a serious study of the historical Jesus.[3] Nam-
ing Schleiermacher as the initiator of the quest for an
understanding of the true historical Plato, Jaeger writes:
"The trend of this approach was towards seeing Plato, who
had become a mighty figure detached from time and history, within his own social background, and making him a
real, solid, historical character." The accomplishment and
the undoing of the liberal historians was to fit a long-
idealized Jesus back into his own social and historical
milieu.

Again, not only superficial liberal Protestants used Jesus
for their own purposes. The great Russian novelist Dostoevsky, who nowadays is often claimed as one of the early
Christian existentialists and a forerunner of our neo-orthodox theologians, treated the historical Jesus in a typically
liberal Protestant fashion. In the famous Grand Inquisitor

[2] W. H. Auden: "The Fallen City," *Encounter*, November 1959.
[3] See Jaeger: *Paideia*, II, p. 78, and Schweitzer: *Quest*, p. 62.

scene of *The Brothers Karamazov,* Dostoevsky also conjured up an unhistorical Jesus to haunt the authoritarian Christians of his day. One of the novelist's greatest political phobias was that the Roman Catholic Church he so detested would conspire with the growing socialist and Communist movements of the late nineteenth century. These political premonitions Dostoevsky expressed in his little-known column "A Writer's Diary," published first while he was editor of the weekly *Grazhdanin,* and later independently. His accounts, according to one commentator, made "the flesh of his readers creep with the bogeys of Communism and Roman Catholicism (whose hidden hand he detected everywhere)." [4] In order to preserve his power in the face of the growing socialist movement, the Pope, wrote Dostoevsky, would have to be "prepared to deny Christ and believe in the human ant heap." [5] The Papists, he wrongly predicted, would unite with socialism to oppose freedom, Holy Russia, and the Orthodox faith. In fact, it turned out that socialism united with Holy Russia to oppose freedom, the Papists, and the Orthodox faith. [6]

In the Grand Inquisitor scene Dostoevsky brought to life his political hopes and fears. The Christ that appears in Seville is a symbol of freedom and anti-authoritarianism, starkly opposed to the Inquisitor's "benevolent" suppres-

[4] Gerald Abraham: *Dostoevsky* (London: Gerald Duckworth & Co.; 1936), p. 118.

[5] Ibid., p. 126.

[6] In so far as non-Communist forms of socialism are concerned, it seems to have been the Protestants who united with socialism. See, for example, the early writings of Reinhold Niebuhr and Paul Tillich, and Tillich's recent statement that "there can be nothing beyond religious socialism." See also the accounts in the Tillich and Niebuhr volumes of the "Library of Living Theology."

sion of freedom. Although the implications of the scene are manifoldly ambiguous, one of them is plain: in order to unite with socialism, the Roman Catholic church would have to abandon the historical Jesus. So even Dostoevsky, "forerunner of present-day Christian existentialism," invoked Jesus' aid in a cultural battle against socialism.

Although the Protestant liberals in America more often took Christ for an ally in their battle *for* a kind of socialism, their approach was, on a more fundamental level, the same as Dostoevsky's: Christ was to be man's helper and guide in his battle against social evil, however that evil might be conceived.

All interpretations—scientific, historical, or literary—are impregnated with theories and prejudices, very often unconsciously held. In order to be criticized, or even to be open to criticism, these principles of interpretation must be brought to light. If the principles, once revealed, stand up to criticism, we may continue to use them, now consciously. If they break down, they should be abandoned or at least used more carefully. The achievement of Schweitzer and his predecessors was to display the unconscious principles on which the liberal interpretation of Jesus was based, and to show—in the light of advancing historical knowledge—that many of these were untenable.

I I I

T H E
New Protestant Thought

O God, grant us the serenity to accept
What cannot be changed;
The courage to change what can be changed;
And the wisdom to know one from the other.
REINHOLD NIEBUHR

For every evil under the sun,
There is a remedy, or there is none.
If there be one, try to find it;
If there be none, never mind it.
MOTHER GOOSE

1 · *On the Border*

WHEN a position runs into recalcitrant facts, some adjustment needs to be made. Sometimes the simplest thing is to deny the facts, a policy for which theologians have traditionally shown some talent. Such a course was hardly open to the Protestant liberals, who had for many years been accusing anti-Darwinian fundamentalists of doing just that. Confronted with a historical Jesus whose person and message were, at least in any straightforward sense, both illiberal and irrational, the Protestant liberals had to face squarely a new and rather formidable question: *Was Jesus himself one of those nonessential historical shells one could in principle discard during the search for the essence of the Christian message?*

A negative answer to this question had of course been tacitly assumed all along. But now, for the first time, Protestant theologians became consciously aware that the various attempts to state the *essence of the Christian message* were subordinate to the question of the *essence of being a Christian.* And a truly Christian identity, it was plausibly argued, demanded assent to the person of the historical Jesus—as he actually had been, not as one might have liked him to be. To the extent that honest identification with the rationalist tradition required that one withhold assent from the newly discovered historical Jesus, it became impossible for a man to be, in good conscience, both a Protestant Christian and a rationalist.

So, contrary to a familiar interpretation of the shift away from Protestant liberalism, the choice was not between Protestant liberalism and neo-orthodoxy. Protestant Christian liberalism had become intellectually impossible. Rather, the choice that confronted Protestant thinkers who were aware what was at stake was between (1) a non-Christian liberal rationalism, which lacked the essential characteristic of Christian identity, assent to the person of the historical Jesus, and (2) a newly self-conscious Christian Protestantism resolved to hold fast to Jesus no matter how irrational a policy that might turn out to be.

This is one of the most important reasons for the intellectual and numerical strength of antiliberal forces within Protestantism today. Since it was almost impossible to put up a serious case for thoroughgoing liberalism *within* Prot-

estant Christianity, those liberal rationalists who wished to
be able to discard anything that conflicted with rational
principles had to abandon Christianity. And those who held
fast to Christ had to be illiberal or uncritical at least about
Christ, however critical they might be on other matters.
This development, although its significance may not have
been fully appreciated at the time it occurred, may prove to
have been the most decisive turning point in the intellectual
history of Protestantism.

With the breakdown of Protestant liberalism, then, the
long marriage of the rationalist tradition and Protestantism
came to an end. Some marriages end in death or separation;
this one ended in a carefully documented divorce. The essence of being a Christian was written into the constitution
of the new ecumenical movement, whose members were
required to agree that "Jesus Christ is Lord." Leonard
Hodgson has chronicled in his Gifford Lectures one important episode of the court proceedings:

> In the summer of 1937 the World Conference on
> Faith and Order and the Universal Christian Council
> for Life and Work had agreed to unite in forming the
> World Council of Churches. In May 1938 there was a
> meeting at Utrecht in Holland for the purpose of
> drawing up a constitution for the proposed Council.
> The Faith and Order Movement had always been a
> Conference of churches 'which accept our Lord Jesus
> Christ as God and Saviour,' . . . The Life and Work
> Movement had never had this restriction, and I was ex-
> pecting the Council to be constituted on its wider
> scale, with the narrower basis written into its constitu-

tion as a requirement for its Faith and Order activities. But speaker after speaker, representing a wide variety of churches from America, Great Britain, Germany, Scandinavia and elsewhere, demanded the acceptance of the Nicene Faith as the basis of the Council itself. I took care to point out that this was not demanded by the Movement I represented as the price of our adherence. It became abundantly clear that this basis would be adopted, not because of any desire to conciliate the stalwarts of the Faith and Order Movement, but because it was the almost unanimous demand of all those present. One speaker voiced the mind of the meeting when he said that if it was intended to have a Council of Christian Churches they must be Christian churches, and Christian churches are churches which accept the Nicene Faith.

The prevailing impression made on my mind was that the debate registered the change that had come over the theological world since I had begun my theological studies in 1913. There was no one present to voice the modernist liberalism which would almost certainly have been a prominent, if not the dominant, force in any similar gathering held a quarter of a century earlier.[1]

If the voice of liberalism had stopped speaking out at the church's conferences, it had not yet stopped pestering the consciences of the church's theologians. For the choice be-

[1] Hodgson: *For Faith and Freedom* (Oxford: Basil Blackwell; 1956), Vol. I, pp. 13 ff. For New Testament support for the position, see Romans 10:9; I Corinthians 8:6; 12:3; II Corinthians 4:5; Philippians 2:11; Colossians 2:6–8.

tween rationalism and Protestant Christianity was not easy or pleasant for most of those compelled to make it. If, on one hand the new Protestant position offered considerable relief, on the other hand it opened new and agonizing dilemmas.

Some relief came from the new definiteness it provided. A basically negative and eliminative spirit like that of Protestant liberalism was bound to leave a religion in a weakened position. For example, its refusal to take up a dogmatic position that could be easily understood and followed by the masses—at a time of rapid industrial growth in mass society—placed Protestant liberalism in danger of committing suicide. Among the critics of Protestantism who noticed this kind of weakness was John Henry Cardinal Newman, the great nineteenth-century British convert to Roman Catholicism. In his "Discourses to Mixed Congregations," he described the Protestants as "children tossed to and fro, and carried about by every gale of doctrine." He added: "If they had faith, they would not change."

Another, more ominous complaint came from Karl Barth. Deploring the practical difficulties graduates of liberal theological faculties faced in conducting their ministries, Barth attributed the trouble to religious individualism, to the Kantian and liberal idea of relying on the internal admonitions of the conscience, rather than on external authority, for moral and spiritual guidance.

Whosoever keeps himself to "modern" theology [wrote Barth] must know that the question is: to be or not to be. For science deprives him of that entire historical outfit of ideas and concepts which were the "motive and quietive" of the religion of the past. . . . For whosoever wants to speak to others only of that which in his own life has become cause or effect of faith, is confronted by the Scylla of clericalism which offers more than it has, and by the Charybdis of agnosticism, which offers nothing at all. But both stand threateningly before us younger theologians, and to this I attribute our immaturity, our surprisingly small enthusiasm for religious activism.[2]

Writing about "Modernism and Christianity," George Santayana observed:

What would make the preaching of the gospel utterly impossible would be the admission that it had no authority to proclaim what has happened or what is going to happen, either in this world or in another.[3]

Protestant liberalism in effect had given up all claim to such authority. The new thought, by drawing a limit to change, tried to regain some of its lost authority.

But the new thought also deeply troubled many of its leaders; and their writings record the intensity of their personal struggles over the matter. Paul Tillich strikes a representative tone when he writes of those who "have found that they were not what they believed themselves to be, even after a deeper level had appeared to them below the vanishing surface. That deeper level itself became surface, when a still deeper level was discovered." [4] The "concept of

[2] Barth: "Moderne Theologie und Reichgottesarbeit," op. cit.
[3] *Winds of Doctrine*, p. 32.
[4] Tillich: *The Shaking of the Foundations* (New York: Charles Scribner's Sons; 1948), p. 56.

the border," Tillich has written elsewhere, is the "fitting symbol for the whole of my personal and intellectual development. It has been my fate, however, in almost every direction, to stand between alternative possibilities of existence, to be completely at home in neither, to take no definitive stand against either." [5]

In Tillich, as in most other eminent Protestants, and indeed as in any *homo religiosus* or *philosophicus*, the problems of self-identity and integrity are fused and chronic. "The chosen young man," Erikson has written:

> extends the problem of his identity to the borders of existence in the known universe; other human beings bend all their efforts to adopt and fulfill the departmentalized identities which they find prepared in their communities. He can permit himself to face as permanent the trust problem which drives others in whom it remains or becomes dominant into denial, despair, and psychosis. . . . others hide in the folds of whatever tradition they are part of because of membership, occupation, or special interests. . . . others must look to their memories, to legends, or to books to find models for the present and the future in what their predecessors have said and done. No wonder that he is something of an old man (a *philosophus*, and a sad one) when his age-mates are young, or that he remains something of a child when they age with finality.[6]

Torn as they were between Christian allegiance and allegiance to reason, it is not surprising that most of the theo-

[5] Tillich: *The Interpretation of History* (New York: Charles Scribner's Sons; 1936), p. 3; see also p. 40 ff.

[6] Erikson: *Young Man Luther*, pp. 261 ff.

logians who like Tillich remained Christians attempted to develop a compromise Christian theology that, although basically irrational, would nevertheless be as rational a form of irrationalism as possible.

Although these attempts differ widely, a certain pattern is common to most of them. On the one hand, they show a dramatic flexibility: any statement of the essence of the Christian *message* is taken to be *in principle* revisable. There is never again to be any fundamentalist adherence to a fixed interpretation of the Christian message, whether Protestant liberal or old Calvinist. Neo-orthodoxy is by no means neo-rigidity. On the other hand, there is an equally dramatic definition of the *limits* of this far-ranging flexibility within a basic inflexibility: whatever his message might turn out to be, assent to Jesus is required. It is a tribute, however, to the real flexibility of the reaction to Protestant liberalism that almost the *only* thing its members are generally agreed on is this assent to Jesus Christ. Many doors are opened; one door is closed. Christian identity is defined in terms of commitment to the messenger, not to some interpretation of his message. Claims to knowledge about God are exchanged for faith in Christ.

2 · *Enter Karl Barth*

The brilliant Swiss theologian Karl Barth forged the basic ideas undergirding the ingenious compromises that enabled some liberally inclined people to remain Protestant. Most contemporary theologians, from Emil Brunner at one extreme to Tillich at the other, are in rather serious disagreement with Barth—not always to the credit of their intellectual and strategical sensitivity. Yet even where they differ from him most radically, they usually owe to his writings their principal concepts and the way they state their problems.

Barth wove into a web of amazing complexity of detail, yet beautiful simplicity of structure, an acute denunciation of the basic errors of liberalism and an elegantly appealing alternative approach. Given his intentions and his commitments, it is hard to imagine a more skillful intellectual solution. He is one of the most interesting, as well as one of the most learned, self-critical, and bold writers in the history of Christian thought—despite the fact that he is profoundly wrong.

Barth first outlined his main ideas in his famous *Römerbrief*, a commentary on St. Paul's *Epistle to the Romans* which was written during World War I. He has expanded, developed, changed, and corrected them in his later works, particularly in his massive, multivolumed *Church Dogmatics*. Here it will be possible to review briefly only a few of his main concepts and point to some of the difficulties in them; but this will be sufficient at least to show what is meant by the phrase, "as rational a form of irrationalism as possible." My basic objection to Barth's thought, which involves the absolute irrational commitment on which he bases his theory, is a matter to return to later.

Beginning with the assumption or commitment that Revelation "happened" in Jesus, Barth resolves to take the assumption seriously in order to trace its implications. Some of the more important of these implications are:

(1) Apologetic theology must be rejected as both useless

and irreverent. It is *useless* because if the Word of God has really been accepted as such it is superfluous to offer reasons for so doing. Moreover, neither those who are forever damned nor those who are to be redeemed could arrive at commitment to the Word of God either by themselves or through the effort of all the apologetic theologians in the world. One might say that Barth believes some men are boxes, forever sealed unto themselves, and that others are cameras, able in principle to receive God's light. But even in the latter cases only God can open the shutter. The gift of faith is a miracle that is entirely in God's hands.

Apologetic theology is *irreverent* because the only proper attitude toward what one has accepted as the Word of God is awe, trust, and obedience. One should accept the Word as the command of God, not try to apologize for it on the dubious liberal grounds that it "works" or agrees with human nature. If it is *God's* word, one does not necessarily compliment it by saying, as the liberals did, that it agrees with mere *human* nature.

(2) But if theology is not to argue on behalf of Christian commitment, what is its task? Barth thinks it has two main jobs, either of which can begin only when commitment to the Word of God has already been made.[7] These are the *description* of the Word to which one is committed, and the *criticism and testing* of other descriptions, past and current.

(3) This is no return, however, to fundamentalism. By "Word of God" Barth does not simply mean "The Bible." The Word of God denotes the revelatory *historical event* to which the Bible bears witness. The locus of religious au-

[7] Barth: *Church Dogmatics* (Edinburgh: T. & T. Clark; 1936), Vol. I., Part 1, pp. 2 ff.

thority, to which commitment is made, is thus removed from the Bible to the historical event behind it.[8]

(4) Hence the Bible itself can be regarded as only a report about and testimony to the Word of God, as revealed through Christ. And like all human reports, the Bible is subject to error. Not only is it true that *we* may misunderstand the Bible; even those who wrote it may have misinterpreted the revelatory event which they had observed.

(5) So all theological statements—that is, statements *about* the Word of God—including those in the Bible, those in the Creeds, those spoken in the pulpits of the churches, and those articulated in theological systems about the essence of Christianity, from the Church Fathers to the Protestant liberals, are subject to constant revision and testing against the Word of God.

All theological statements, that is, are forever *conjectures* about the Word of God.[9] We can never know whether or not our statements do in fact express the truth about the Word of God or whether they are mixed with error stemming from our misinterpretations, or from our conscious or unconscious imposition of our own presuppositions on the historical event. "As a theological discipline," Barth writes on the first page of his *Church Dogmatics*, "Dogmatics is the scientific test to which the Christian Church puts herself regarding the language about God which is peculiar to her." Theology has a continuing critical task; correction of dogma is to be expected.

[8] See *Church Dogmatics*, Vol. I, Part 2, p. 863, for a discussion by Barth of his disagreements with the fundamentalists.

[9] Barth also uses the words "essay" and "hypothesis" to describe theological statements and the character of dogma. See *Church Dogmatics* Vol. I, Part 2, p. 730.

(6) The Word of God, however, is the *only* criterion to which theological statements need conform, the only standard in respect to which they may be criticized. Although all of us, to be sure, approach any document with a store of interpretational principles, in a clash it is *our* principles which must yield.[1] God's Word and Commandment to men "stands in judgment" on their prideful speculations and is to be accepted and obeyed, whatever the devilish promptings of contemporary thought. "It cannot be otherwise than that Dogmatics runs counter to every philosophy no matter what form it may have assumed," Barth warned in his *Credo*.[2]

In other words, argues Barth, if it is improper to challenge a scientific statement on the ground that it does not conform with the Word of God it is also improper to challenge a theological statement on the ground that it does not conform to scientific demands.[3]

Thus, Barth's methodology helps explain the breakdown of past statements about the true identity or essence of Christianity and allows for the possibility that all such statements will eventually be revised. It does this by removing the locus of faith from any particular statement of the essence to the historical fact that lies behind all such statements. "The question of truth," he writes, "with which

---

[1] *Church Dogmatics*, Vol. I, Part 2, pp. 728–33.

[2] Loc. cit., p. 186. See also *Church Dogmatics*, Vol. I, Part 2, p. 730, and Vol. III, Part 1, pp. 343 ff.

[3] Yet Barth does not believe that science and theology ever in fact conflict. It is, he implies, only a *philosophy* of science which can conflict with theology. See *Kirchliche Dogmatik* (Zollikon-Zürich: Evangelischer Verlag; 1948), Vol. III, Part 2. But see my comments on the instrumentalist view of science which makes this view possible, in section 5 of this chapter.

theology is throughout concerned, is the question as to the agreement between the language about God peculiar to the Church and the essence of the Church . . . which is Jesus Christ." [4] The essence of being a Christian is submission to the essence of the Church, which is Jesus Christ.

The same Barthian methodology has made the ecumenical movement possible by providing a general formula in terms of which Christians who are absolutely committed to the Word of God but who differ about the less important matter of the interpretation of the content of the Word of God may work together. [5]

To sum up, Barth has given an answer to the question of what are the boundaries of change and belief and of criticism within Christianity. His answer is that a Christian may abandon any statement about the *content* of the Christian message—on the ground that it is an inadequate statement of what the message really is—but he may not, *as a Christian*, abandon the Christian identity, the essence of being a Christian, which is submission to the authority of the Word of God, whatever its content may turn out to be. Christians, for Barth, are those people who interpret the Word of God and do not ask whether It is true, but only whether any statement about It is a true statement about the Word of God.

For anyone who begins with the assumption—or the commitment—that final revelation happened in a particular historical event, Barth's is the best theory I know about how

[4] *Church Dogmatics*, Vol. I, Part 1, p. 3.
[5] See William Hamilton: "On Doing Without Knowledge of God," *Journal of Religion*, January 1957. Hamilton argues that Christians can only speak of the "minimum that is left" by telling the stories of their lives to one another.

to approach the task of determining the content of that revelation.

But for many of us the difficulty lies in the initial irrational assumption or commitment. We wish to question the truth of the Word of God. And that in itself puts us outside Barth's Church. We are either sealed boxes or cameras as yet unused; there is no way to tell which.

There are, of course, other problems in Barth's thought which we can subject to analysis without leaving the circle of the faithfully committed—in particular, the formidable one of how far it is possible for us to test conjectures, especially genuinely new ones, about an event that has disappeared into the irrecoverable past. Barth's difficulty here has wrongly been compared with Bacon's. Bacon's mistake was to believe that the experiential reports he sought in order to test scientific theories and eradicate prejudices of scientists would themselves be free from prejudice and theory, so that he could read Nature straight, as it were. This mistake Barth avoids: he acknowledges that even his best experiential reports about the Word of God—those found in the New Testament—are themselves impregnated with interpretation, theory, and prejudice.

On the other hand, the natural experimenter who abandons the notion that his sense experiences are given and incorrigible can go on to test his sense experiences themselves by further tests. But the only sense experiences that could have helped criticize our reports of the historical event which Barth calls the Word of God—those of other contemporaries of Jesus—are now as far beyond recall as the event itself.

3 · Gestalt Theology

Many of Barth's fellow theologians—Brunner, Bultmann, Niebuhr, Tillich—were unable to follow him all the
way into the extreme theological purism of describing what
the Word of God says without trying to relate it to contemporary philosophical and scientific thinking. In the face of
the breakdown of rationalizing and accommodating Protestant Liberalism, these men found themselves in a situation rather analogous to that of the post-Humean empiricists who in the search for material substance stripped away
all the perceivable properties of material objects only to
find—to their surprise!—that nothing perceivable remained. After the Christian ethic and the liberal picture of
Jesus had been discarded, no obvious rationally defensible
candidate was left in terms of which Christian commitment
might be explained.

Even when it had been agreed to identify Christianity by
a formula; that is, to accept that the essence of being a
Christian was assent to Christ, there remained the question
of what assenting to Christ amounted to. Was there in the
Bible no unique and reasonable message that could be
called, even in a conjectural way, the message of Christianity, despite the breakdown of all the obvious candidates for
such a keystone position? If such a message did exist, the
formula could at least be explicated in terms of it.

And if no such message existed, what would remain of
Protestant Christianity beyond a highly confused, loosely
knit political alliance of traditional organizations whose
members grasped at shadows of shadows—a world as con-

fused and chaotic as that of the empirical philosophers, with their bundles and jumbles of sense impressions?

If the character of the Jesus to whom assent was required was indefinite, and if commitment to Jesus was required *no matter what* Jesus was and did, the threat was that only the subjective Protestant commitment would be definite. Its object would be an "I know not what and I care not what"—hardly a satisfactory object of worship for anyone who regards religion as more than a series of bows and ceremonies, who seeks a personal identity in the Protestant tradition.

For example, H. R. Niebuhr, after defining a Christian in a typical neo-orthodox way as "one who counts himself as belonging to that community of men for whom Jesus Christ —his life, words, deeds, and destiny—is of supreme importance as the key to the understanding of themselves and their world," goes on wistfully to remark that the variety of personal and communal beliefs in Jesus Christ is so great, and the interpretation of his essential nature so manifold, "that the question must arise whether the Christ of Christianity is indeed one Lord." [6]

When Peer Gynt asked: "What is this question of being one's self?" the Button Molder replied that it was to "follow the Master's intention." When Peer insisted: "But suppose one was never told what the Master's intention was?" the Button Molder answered: "One must have insight." [7] Many contemporary theologians have tried to provide such insight through a kind of gestalt approach: if one stands back from the details of the text, takes the Bible as a whole,

[6] Niebuhr: *Christ and Culture*, pp. 11–12.
[7] Henrik Ibsen: *Peer Gynt*, Act V, scene 9.

and reads beneath the surface, one finds remaining a
"Christian vision of man," a "Christian interpretation of
history," a "Biblical *Weltanschauung*," "permanent symbols," a "Christian epistemology," or something of the sort.
All these ideas are materials for a rationally defensible
content for Protestant commitment. They are not themselves put forth as essential; if *they* broke down, they could
be abandoned with impunity. But in the all-important
meantime, they would provide content to the nonabandon-
able commitment to Christ.

Although these attempts have been, I believe, fundamentally unsuccessful, they are often extremely interesting.
There is, after all, at least one sense in which the Bible does,
to use Barth's phrase, "stand in judgment" on us all: it is a
magnificent record of high-level human experience, a part
of our tradition which is very hard to live up to. Since contemporary culture is as prone as its predecessors to dally
with superficialities, the material found in the Bible might
deepen, and often correct, modern approaches to certain
standard human problems.

Reinhold Niebuhr is one of the most stimulating of the
contemporary plunderers of Biblical wisdom. The words
"stimulating" and "plunderer" are used advisedly. For
Niebuhr *is* stimulating: his remarks on intellectual and
political history, on contemporary politics, on psychology,
are often brilliantly perceptive. And yet the use he makes
of his insights does amount to a kind of piracy.

If reading the Bible animates Niebuhr's thinking, one
can only be glad for him. Even the most methodologically
minded psychologist does not depend on the accumulation
of data to reach his discoveries or achieve his insights. He

can use any method that helps him—from immersion in literature, to Bible reading, to swallowing amphetamine—to achieve insight. And there is, of course, no guarantee that any of these will work. The scientific method comes in *later*, when he subjects his visions to test in order to determine whether they correspond to fact or are just exciting ideas. Niebuhr is not always sufficiently critical of his ideas, but at least he presents them in an unpretentious way.

Another good example of this gestalt method can be found in the late Michael Foster's book *Mystery and Philosophy*. Foster thought that he had discovered in the Bible a theory of knowledge far superior to the Hellenist theories of knowledge which culminated in twentieth-century positivism. Arguing that the Biblical theory provided a corrective on precisely those epistemological points where the Hellenist theories broke down, Foster pointed out that the Hellenist tradition had tended to maintain that "the riddle does not exist," that there is no ultimate mystery in the world, that there is a *method for attaining certainty* which at least some men can operate. Such positivist views, as Foster knew, had been undermined quite independently of any criticism from theologians.

In contrast to the Hellenic idea of "unhiddenness" of Being, Foster argued, the Biblical view maintains that God is hidden. The Israelites held no simple belief in the capacity of human reason to penetrate the mystery of ultimate reality, or in the "self-disclosure of Being" to the contemplating mind. According to the Israelites, man must *wait upon* God for a revelation; according to the Greeks, man can reach Him by himself, by mastering the technique.

One can agree with Foster in rejecting what he calls the

Hellenic view; it is less certain that *his* Biblical view of epistemology is indeed *the* Biblical view. But the acceptable parts of the theory he expounds—and most parts of it are acceptable—are not uniquely Biblical. They correspond very closely to the pre-Socratic emphasis on mystery, the "hiddenness of truth," and the conjectual nature of knowledge.[8]

Interesting as such attempts are, some questions must be raised about them. In the first place, thinkers like Niebuhr and Foster tend quite arbitrarily to identify a true view which is found in the Bible with *the* Biblical view. In fact, there are a variety of competing Biblical views on most subjects; and no theologian so far has provided any method for discriminating between the Biblical views that are found in the Bible and the non-Biblical views that, embarrassingly enough, are also found in the Bible. Walter Kaufmann, in his brilliant *Critique of Religion and Philosophy*, has given many examples which illustrate this point.[9]

The method of contemporary theologians can often be reduced to three rather simple steps: (1) Run through the Bible picking out profound ideas about certain contemporary problems. (2) Run through contemporary secular lit-

---

[8] I discussed this point with Foster at Oxford in the summer of 1959, shortly before his death. He told me that the pre-Socratic Greek philosophers had not occurred to him when he called the view he opposed the "Hellenic" view. He was thinking of the tradition, and the "quest for certainty," which began with Plato and Aristotle. See Foster: *Mystery and Philosophy* (London: SCM Press Ltd.; 1957) and *Mind*, 1934, pp. 446 ff; 1935, pp. 439 ff; and 1936, pp. 1 ff. Compare Foster's remarks with Tillich: *Protestant Era*, pp. 30–1; and Popper: "Back to the Pre-Socratics," op. cit.

[9] Kaufmann: *Critique* (New York: Harper & Brothers; 1958), especially chapter 6.

erature picking out superficialities concerning these same problems. (3) Match the two in a book, thus providing an easy demonstration of the superiority of the Bible and the Christian tradition to contemporary secular culture. The basic unsoundness of the approach is aggravated by the ambiguity with which the results are often presented. If one interprets them one way, they seem undeniable commonplaces. If one interprets them another way, they seem ridiculous. Much of the appeal, as well as the apparent novelty and profundity, of the theological commentary depends on its talent for bestriding two horses at once—sometimes even when they are galloping in opposite directions.

Another question concerns the significance of the undoubted presence of a great deal of wisdom in the Bible. Many contemporary theologians do little more than list and elaborate on the wisdom contained in the Bible as if thereby to establish the superiority of Christianity. Such a numerical approach, being a kind of stepdaughter of the old argument for design, need only be formulated to be rejected by almost any theologian. But, of course, the assumption is not usually formulated.

Although Niebuhr, along with most other neo-orthodox thinkers, has been disturbed by the rift between reason and Christian commitment, the disturbance has not gone very deep philosophically. The theologian who seems to have been most disturbed on a deep philosophical level, and who has also made the most elaborate attempt to combine commitment to reason with commitment to Jesus the Christ, is Paul Tillich, to whose ideas I wish now to turn.

4 · *Paul Tillich and Objective Truth*

The late R. G. Collingwood once wrote that it was impossible to reconstruct historically or intellectually anything that had failed: be it the strategy of the losing side in a battle or of the thought of a philosopher who had been unable to solve his problems.[1] Collingwood was not only wrong here; his own archaeological researches in the history of Roman Britain refute his statement. Yet a study of Tillich's writings helps one appreciate how Collingwood could have come to such a conclusion. Tillich gives the impression that what he is trying to say is of vital importance. But it is difficult to determine just what he has said, let alone measure his success.

Behind this obscurity, however, some problems and ideas do lie. Like his spiritual colleagues, Tillich has seen that many traditional Christian concepts—such as that of original sin, echoing as it does in Freudian psychology—have not outworn their usefulness. His first task, then, is to restate and redefine such concepts, with the hope of eliminating their supernatural features and of bringing their valid aspects into focus. "You must first save concepts," he once wrote, "before you can save souls." [2] Specifically, his strategy is to point up certain contemporary human problems—classified under the five headings of rationality, finitude,

---

[1] Robin George Collingwood: *An Autobiography* (London: Oxford University Press; 1939), pp. 69–70.

[2] Tillich: "The Existentialist Challenge and the Religious Answer," speech delivered at Darmouth College, Great Issues Course, May 11, 1953, p. 7 (mimeographed). See also Tillich's "Introductory Remarks" to his *Dynamics of Faith* (New York: Harper and Brothers; 1957).

sin, unity, destiny—and to show that certain Biblical themes—which can be grouped under the five concepts of Revelation, God, Christ, Holy Spirit, and Kingdom of God —provide, when interpreted in a certain way, important insights into these problems.[3]

To give a simple example of how this approach can work: Niebuhr's doctrine of original sin could possibly be reinterpreted on Tillichian lines somewhat as follows.[4] The Genesis story of Adam's original sin—for which God is said to be punishing the subsequent generations of men—can be understood in part as a primitive explanation of the fact that there is evil already in the world when any of us arrive here: "structural evil," which is "there," beyond our control. Each child that is born this year will grow up in a world torn by war which he is in no way responsible for bringing about but which will condition his daily life and perhaps even lead him to personal destruction. Other children will inherit the diseases of their parents; still others, their parents' economic plight or broken marriages. Even where the original situation can be corrected externally, scars often remain in the form of neuroses. We are unable by ourselves to cure all the ills we are born with. If healing does occur, it is often more a matter of luck—the theologian might say "grace"—than of our own efforts.[5]

Tillich tries to preserve such acceptable implications in the old concepts and to disarm the supernatural and magical aspects that are no longer tenable, such as—on a very ele-

[3] The five Biblical concepts just named correspond to the five parts of Tillich's system.

[4] See Tillich: *The Protestant Era*, pp. xx, 165.

[5] Ibid., p. xxi.

mentary level—the belief that God actually punished a fellow named Adam for eating an apple. The result is a "broken myth," symbolically true. Tillich's practice up to this point has won him many admirers, and thus far, his procedure is largely acceptable.

Right here, however, an extremely important problem arises for all recent Christian apologetical theologians. Namely, other faiths—not to mention literature, such as Greek tragedy and Shakespeare, and ordinary folklore— also possess symbols and myths embodying important truths about the way men should confront life. What, then, is to preserve the claims of Christianity to religious superiority? What is to mark off the "true faith" of Christianity from competing faiths?

Many contemporary theologians do not even try to face this question; when it is raised, they appeal to their original commitment to Christ. Similarly, the presence of a treasure of wisdom in the Bible is not usually religiously significant except to the person who has already committed himself to Christ but whose faith is not firm enough to dispense with such buttressing.

To Tillich's credit, he does face the question. In answer, he maintains that the Christian tradition contains, in a unique way, a symbol that satisfies what he calls "the Protestant principle." The Protestant principle, a rather primitive attempt on Tillich's part to define a principle of criticism—indeed, the principle of criticism which he believes is the *criterion* of "objectively true faith"—is that no man or institution possesses the ultimate truth. To satisfy this principle, a symbol must "express the ultimate which is really ultimate" by implying its own "lack of ultimacy."

Such symbols, then, are themselves not permanently valid or unrevisable; what is most important is something beyond themselves to which they are "pointing."

At its very center, Tillich claims, the Christian religion possesses just such a symbol. Jesus, by sacrificing himself on the cross, indicated his own lack of ultimacy as a historical figure. Hence, for Tillich, the religion whose central symbol is Christ's cross is, when the Calvary event is properly interpreted, the "objectively true faith."

Three important questions arise here:

(1) How does Tillich know that the symbols of an objectively true faith will be those which imply their own lack of ultimacy?

(2) Suppose he is right. Does the Calvary event, as Tillich maintains, really provide such a symbol?

(3) Suppose it does. Is this the only such symbol? Do such symbols appear only in Christianity? Or do other religions also possess them? And if they do, how does Tillich's answer meet the original problem of distinguishing Protestant Christianity as the most meritorious religion?

These questions may be considered in turn.

(1) Tillich's answer to the first question leads to the topic of definitions. That an "objectively true faith" will "imply its own lack of ultimacy" simply follows from Tillich's definition of an objectively true faith. But, then, even if Christianity *were* the only religion possessing such a symbol, the matter would still rest on an arbitrary definition. The whole issue of Christianity's superiority would

turn not on fact or on a point of view but on a stipulation. Moreover, even if it should be agreed that any objectively true faith will "imply its own lack of ultimacy" in some sense, it hardly follows that any faith which implies its own lack of ultimacy is an objectively true faith.

(2) But suppose that Tillich's definition were in some sense acceptable. Does the Calvary event, as Tillich argues, provide such an objectively true symbol? Unfortunately, it does not satisfy his definition in any clear way. Jesus did indeed sacrifice his person to the cause to which he was dedicated and to what he thought was God. In so doing, he can be said to have sacrificed himself for the "ultimate beyond himself." But the question arises whether Jesus, in order to act as the incarnation of a principle that is intended as a principle of criticism, would not have had to be willing *to sacrifice not only himself but also his conception of his message.* Was Jesus at all critical of the symbols through which he himself apprehended "the ultimate"? There seems to be nothing in the Gospels to indicate that he was; and independent New Testament scholarship does not seem to disagree, at least on this point. Rather, the Calvary story seems to be that of a man who sacrificed part of himself (his life) for the sake of a greater cause but who never sacrificed or seemed willing to sacrifice or seemed even slightly critical of that other part of himself—his message—for the sake of an ultimate truth beyond that message. To put it less sympathetically, Jesus sacrificed his life but not his delusion.[6]

Only if Jesus' conception of his message is identified in

[6] Tillich took a contrary view, but provided no clear supporting arguments. See *Systematic Theology*, Vol. I, p. 136

advance with the ultimate truth does he satisfy Tillich's definition. Certain other features of Tillich's thought, however, would prevent him from equating Jesus' own conception of his message with the ultimate truth.

(3) But suppose we overlook such objections and assume that Jesus does fulfill Tillich's definition. Do other non-Christian religions contain no symbols that also satisfy the definition and thus qualify as symbols of the "objectively true faith"?

That there are such symbols in other religions can be easily shown. I shall do so in a roundabout way—one that should incidentally bring out the dangers inherent in procedures like Tillich's—by comparing Tillich's program with that of the logical positivists, which I believe was equally misguided. My aim here, as it was in dealing with the second question, is to show that even if one were to accept Tillich's definition, his system would *still* break down.

As Tillich wished to demarcate true faith from its competitors, so the positivists wished to demarcate true science from its rivals—pseudo-science, metaphysics, and especially theology. Any statement, at least in earlier positivism, had to be logical, scientific, or meaningless. One would determine to which of the latter two categories a non-logical statement belonged by establishing whether it could be verified. At first some positivists claimed that this criterion simply recorded a fact about the world. Later they too admitted that it was just a definition, or—as they preferred to say—a "stipulation."

The positivists were intellectually routed as early as 1931, when Professor Popper of the University of London, then a young Viennese physicist, showed the positivists of the famous Vienna Circle that their criterion of meaning would not work. He pointed out that according to their criterion *all scientific laws were meaningless.*[7] Later he showed that "arch-metaphysical assertions" about an omnipotent and omniscient creature (such as a god) *are* meaningful *on the positivists' criterion.*[8] One *could* demarcate science from pseudo-science (such as astrology) and religion; but not through a criterion of meaningfulness. Theology (like astrology) might be untenable—and it was certainly unscientific—but it was not necessarily meaningless. Positivism, hence, not only was objectionable philosophically; it could not even account for science, let alone support it!

Tillich's program can be criticized in a parallel way. Not only is it philosophically objectionable; it doesn't even benefit Protestantism. Many non-Christian symbols fit Tillich's definition of objectively true faith. Perhaps the clearest example is one the rationalists have always held dear: the death of Socrates. In Tillich's way of speaking, the argument might go something like this: Socrates, who sought throughout his spatio-temporal existence to achieve the Good in his own person, sacrificed his person as Socrates, the embodiment of the Good, to the Good which was beyond himself. For Socrates refused the opportunity to escape the death sentence imposed on him by the tribunals of democratic Athens, lest he deny the Good as it expresses

---

[7] Popper: *Logik der Forschung* (Vienna: Springer Verlag; 1934), translated as *The Logic of Scientific Discovery* (New York: Basic Books; 1959).

[8] Popper: "The Demarcation between Science and Metaphysics," *The Philosophy of Rudolf Carnap*, ed. P. A. Schilpp.

itself in a respect for the rule of law in a democracy. Moreover, Socrates was critical of his own conjectures about the nature of the Good.

Now I certainly do not want to deify Socrates. My only point is that, *on Tillich's own definition,* Socrates is as divine as Jesus. If this should seem acceptable to some liberal disciples of Tillich, let them ponder that a similar conclusion could be reached about the Russian state: on Tillich's formal definition, the Russian state can be shown to be as divine as Jesus. The Russian state demands the total surrender of those who accept its claims and offers total fulfillment to its adherents. Therefore, according to Tillich's definition, it is an object of "ultimate concern." It is very much alive; therefore it is "subjectively true" for Tillich. It expresses, at least in theory, its own "lack of ultimacy": the never-never-land of the classless society is said to lie ahead, beyond the dictatorship of the proletariat. The present austerity of the Russian state is a collective sacrifice for the future; its protest against the bourgeois and the capitalistic is an expression of its ultimate commitment to a world without classes. Ultimate commitment to the Russian state is, therefore, objectively true faith, by Tillich's definition. Tillich, then, seems to be one more doctor whose cure is worse than the disease.

Tillich could doubtless evade these objections. He might avoid the counterexample of Socrates, for instance, by *redefining* "objectively true faith" so as to exclude Socrates. By continuously redefining, one can save any system. If in a game of chess one player is allowed to change the rules whenever he is in danger of checkmate, the second player is unlikely ever to win.

Tillich, of course, is not the first to resort to such games-
manship; nor will he be the last. After Einstein presented
his theories of relativity, a number of leading physicists
tried to save Newtonian mechanics in a similar way—by
reinterpreting, redefining, and adjusting the old concepts,
and by introducing auxiliary rules.

If Socrates and Russia were obscure counterexamples
from little-known tribal religions, one could excuse Tillich
for overlooking them. As it is, one can only wonder at his
statements that "Christianity expresses itself in such a
symbol in contrast to all other religions" and "the fact that
this criterion is identical with the Protestant principle and
has become reality in the Cross of the Christ constitutes the
superiority of Protestant Christianity."

The point is important enough to stress. If Tillich could
once admit either that Christ did not provide an incarnation of the Protestant principle or else that his incarnation
of it was not in any clear way special,[9] he would have to give
up either his Protestant principle or his Christianity. In
fact, this is a point about which Tillich has, at least once,
expressed some tentative doubts. In an article published in
1958, he wrote of the encounter of Christianity with other
religions:

I do not think this encounter, which becomes more
concrete and existential every day, has been taken
seriously enough in Christian theology, including my
own system. The statement that Jesus is the Christ and
therefore the incarnation of the universal Logos of
God is a matter of continuous testing, not only in view

[9] But see Tillich: *The Protestant Era*, pp. xi, xix.

of secular culture but also in view of the other world religions.[1]

Tillich's liberality here is, however, tempered and complicated by certain remarks he made earlier—remarks which make it extremely difficult to interpret the statement just quoted. In *The Protestant Era*, for example, Tillich wrote:

> In the power of the New Being that is manifest in Jesus as the Christ . . . the Protestant protest comes to an end. Here is the bedrock on which it stands and *which is not subjected to criticism*. Here is the sacramental foundation of Protestantism, of the Protestant principle and of the Protestant reality.[2]

---

[1] Tillich: "Beyond the Usual Alternatives," *The Christian Century*, May 7, 1958.

[2] Loc. cit., pp. xxii ff. (the italics are mine). On p. 234 Tillich states that the Protestant principle may not be subjected to criticism. See also Martin Luther, who, during his attack on Erasmus, wrote: "A Christian ought . . . to be certain of what he affirms, or else he is not a Christian." (*De Servo Arbitrio*, Werke, Band XVIII [Weimar, 1908], p. 601) and H. A. Hodges's statement: "Not only the content, but also the manner of religious belief is different from that of our belief in the truth of a scientific hypothesis . . . it is the result of reflection on . . . evidence by experts in scientific research; and they put it forward and the layman accepts it from them, always as something provisional, open to revision in the light of fresh evidence which may at any time be found. There may be people in the world who accept the belief in the existence of God in this spirit, but they are probably few in number. Such is not genuine religious belief. Religious belief . . . is held not as a theory which further evidence might modify, but as a fundamental and immutable truth." ("What Is to Become of Philosophical Theology?," *Contemporary British Philosophy* [New York: The Macmillan Company; 1956], p. 229.) For other views on these lines, see H. R. Niebuhr: *The Meaning of Revelation* (New York: The Macmillan Company; 1941), p. 139; and Barth: *Church Dogmatics*, Vol. I, Part 2, pp. 239–40.

If the objections to the claim that Jesus fulfills the Protestant principle in some special way are correct, Tillich's thought is due for some drastic revision. But what happens when positivists or followers of Tillich meet objections like these? For a number of years after their program came under fire, the positivists attempted to make definitional adjustments in their criterion of meaning. Some remnants of this revisionist program are still very much alive, but positivism is for the most part being abandoned; those who were once under its influence today argue a more modest empiricism. Unlike the positivists, however, Tillich and his followers continue spinning definitions and multiplying criteria.

This is certainly not because theologians as individuals tend to be less objective or open-minded than positivists, or because positivists, any more than other people, like to see their pet theories smashed. Philosophers are just as human as theologians; if their sin is more original than that of the theologians, that may be more a matter of intellect than of virtue. Perhaps philosophers generally take a more flexible position than theologians because they are more exposed to internal criticism than are theologians. A part of the game of philosophy is to expose one's theories and those of others to criticism. Philosophers are engaged in following the argument where it leads and in encouraging and listening to criticism; they are members of the critical community. There is criticism within the theological community, too. But it is usually *constructive* criticism—in the worst sense of the word. Its aim is to evade the criticisms of those who are outside the theological circle. Tillich, for example, has said that theologians should emphasize the areas in which they *agree*, not those in which they disagree. This may be good form within the club, but it is not notably helpful in avoiding error.

Reinhold Neibuhr in his later books has championed democracy as the best means developed by man to rid society of bad rulers. But the political aspect is only one side of a broader problem: how to get rid of error whenever and however it appears. The question is whether the structure and institutions of the theological community are such that erroneous ideas can be removed; or whether it is not rather easy for a false idea to entrench itself within theology.

5 · *Philosophical Queries*

The new Protestant thought presents a number of more general difficulties. One of these revolves around the contemporary focus on symbols in theology and in other fields. Behind this concentration of attention is the hope that thereby (often through approaches influenced by Husserl's phenomenology) it will be possible to attain absolute presuppositions or categories of thought. The theologians have failed to see that symbols will not do the job; and this mistake is rather ironical. In their attack on empiricism, the theologians eagerly point out—quite rightly—that sense experience is not "given" but is itself a matter of interpretation, since it is "theory-impregnated." But they have not applied this observation to the *apprehension of symbols*. This can be done as follows: (1) *Symbols* are not "given" either; they do not interpret themselves. (2) We need rules in terms of which to interpret symbols and evaluate and state the claims of any particular symbol. (3) Symbols, then, are *dependent* on interpretational rules. (4) *There-fore, symbols cannot be ultimate, i.e.,* independent, any more than the "given" sense observations of the positivists can be ultimate and incorrigible.[3]

Another, perhaps equally important, difficulty arises from the acceptance, by almost all the theological writers con-cerned, of a conception of the nature of *science* which com-bines phenomenalism, positivism, and instrumentalism. Some of the central tenets of Barth's and Tillich's thought —such as their belief that it is impossible in principle for theological beliefs to conflict with scientific hypotheses— rest on this concept. This conception of science, however, has been refuted.

It has been shown, for example, that although un-testable metaphysical assertions cannot conflict with *re-ports* of *scientific* observation, they *can* conflict with scien-tific hypotheses, or "laws of nature." [4] To be sure, such metaphysical assertions cannot be *disproved* by the fact that they are in conflict with accepted scientific hypotheses— for scientific hypotheses cannot be conclusively verified in the way the positivists would wish. Scientific hypotheses remain forever conjectural (and highly *im*probable, to boot).

This is only one aspect of a broader point. Most twen-

[3] For an application of similar ideas to symbolism in art, see E. H. Gombrich's brilliant book, *Art and Illusion* (New York: Pantheon Books; 1960).

[4] See J. W. N. Watkins's excellent series of articles on this subject: "Between Analytic and Empirical," *Philosophy,* April 1957, especially p. 129; "Confirmable and Influential Metaphysics," *Mind,* July 1958, pp. 345 ff.; and "When Are Statements Empirical?" *British Journal for the Philosophy of Science,* February 1960.

tieth-century religious thinkers, including the Roman
Catholic Pierre Duhem and others, have been able to avoid
the old clash between science and religion by accepting
a view of science which so denatures it that it could not in
principle conflict with metaphysics and religion. These
thinkers strongly disagree with the positivists not over
the *nature* of science but over the positivist claim that there
is no meaningful or legitimate sphere of intellectual activity
beyond "science" interpreted positivistically. This assumption about science is so integral a part of recent
theological thought that much of it would topple were this
view refuted—as it has been.[5] The claim that no conflict
between science and religion is possible is only one of the
ways in which men have tried to solve the conflict between
science and religion.

Within Tillich's own system, in his central concept of
"ultimate concern," the boundary line between science and
religion is not clear. Tillich argues that all men have ultimate concerns, and that one's God is the object of one's
ultimate concern. Several questions arise here: Is the statement that all men have ultimate concerns a psychological
scientific statement subject to empirical refutation? If so,
a major part of Tillich's theological system is in potential
clash with science. If not, what is the status of the claim?
Again, does a person with a "split personality" have an

---

[5] See the articles by Watkins cited in the previous footnote. See also
Popper: "Three Views Concerning Human Knowledge," *Contemporary
British Philosophy*, ed. H. D. Lewis (New York: The Macmillan Company;
1956), and "A Note on Berkeley as Precursor of Mach," *British Journal
for the Philosophy of Science*, May 1953; and Joseph Agassi: "Duhem
versus Galileo," *British Journal for the Philosophy of Science*, November
1957.

ultimate concern? Rather, does not a great deal of the personal neurosis that Tillich stresses result from the fact that men do *not* have some ultimate concern but are inconclusively torn between two or more concerns? David Riesman has observed: "We will find that the same pluralism which exists in the society exists in many of its individuals, and that we are talking to one part of a person and against another." [6]

[6] See his "Values in Context," *The American Scholar*, Vol. 22, No. 1, 1952. For an illustration of how readily other theologians accept a positivist view of science, see Barth: *Church Dogmatics*, Vol. III, Part 1, pp. ix–x; Vol. III, Part 1, p. 344; and Vol. I, Part 1, pp. 7 ff. In the latter, Barth cites Scholz's incorrect discussion of the role of proof in science as embodying the "concept of science for our time."

I V

The Dilemma of Ultimate Commitment and the Rationalist Search for Integrity

1 · *The* Tu Quoque *Argument*

> CONTEMPORARY Christians should support those who relativize world and man.
>
> KARL HEIM [1]

SOME of the dramatic argumentative themes just discussed, which are characteristic features of the writings of such theologians as Tillich, Niebuhr, Brunner, and Bultmann—ideas of sin and symbol, broken myth, and Biblical *Weltanschauung*—are so intriguing and familiar that many people have come to regard them as the most important features of contemporary Protestantism. This is a mistake: as perhaps only Barth has adequately appreciated, such arguments are quite unimportant.

They are unimportant not because, as Barth might say, they are irreverent, but because they are not taken seriously.

---

[1] *Religion and Culture, Essays in Honor of Paul Tillich,* ed. Walter Leibrecht (New York: Harper and Brothers; 1959), p. 194.

Although they are billed as arguments in support of the Christian position, they are not treated as such: when some of these arguments are toppled, the theological edifice they are supposedly buttressing does not even lean. And the fact that a man sees no reason to abandon a position when an argument he put forward to support it is refuted indicates that his position, far from *depending* on the argument, was held independently of it. He may use the argument as a tool to convert others or to exorcise his own doubts; such arguments are the neon lights, not the foundations, of the theological edifice.

Fortunately, this "heads I win, tails you lose" [2] technique for using arguments without taking them seriously can be easily detected most of the time. One need only inquire whether the advocate of a particular position would abandon it if his argument were shown to be false. If he would not, then his position does not depend on that argument; in so far as a serious defense of the position is concerned, the argument is therefore superfluous.

The only serious argument for Christian commitment today is a *tu quoque* argument about the limits of rationality which is rooted in the unsolved philosophical problem I have referred to as "the dilemma of ultimate commitment." This argument is crucial, not only because no one has seemed able to refute it but because the Christian commitment of many Protestants today *does* depend upon it.[3] It does so because the argument provides a *rational*

[2] I owe this apt name to Dr. Joseph Agassi.

[3] For examples, see Heim: *Christian Faith and Natural Science*; David E. Roberts: "Tillich's Doctrine of Man," especially Section III, "The Limitations of Objectivity," in *The Theology of Paul Tillich*, ed. Kegley and Bretall (New York: The Macmillan Company; 1956); *Faith and Logic*,

excuse for irrational commitment. Therefore, if due weight is given to the fact that the dilemma was believed to be inescapable when at the breakdown of Protestant liberalism many theologians decided to remain within the Protestant tradition, we can hardly blame them intellectually for so doing. But if the argument of this and the following chapter is correct; if I succeed in refuting the *tu quoque* argument and solving the problem in which it is rooted, then this excuse will be invalid for future irrational commitment, Protestant or otherwise.

Just what is the powerful *tu quoque* argument? It is that (1) for certain logical reasons, rationality is so limited that *everyone* has to make a dogmatic irrational commitment; (2) therefore, the Christian has a right to make whatever commitment he pleases; and (3) therefore, no one has a right to criticize him for this.

The correctness of the two closely related conclusions, of course, depends on that of the premise about the limits of rationality. This premise—which arises out of the need to stem an infinite regress and from the fact that arbitrary dogmatic commitment seems the only way to do this—can be explained as follows. No matter what belief is advanced, someone can always challenge it with: "How do you know?" and "Give me a reason." Unless this procedure is to go on forever, it must be halted at a "standard," "criterion," "ultimate presupposition," "end," or "goal" whose authority is simply accepted. If all men do not cease their questioning at the same point, however, "ultimate

---

ed. Basil Mitchell (London: George Allen and Unwin; 1957); Alasdair MacIntyre: "The Logical Status of Religious Belief," *Metaphysical Beliefs* (London: SCM Press; 1957).

relativism" results. For there is no Archimedes' lever with which to decide among competing sets of ultimate standards. Even if everyone did happen to stop at the same place, there would be no way to determine whether this universal subjective standard led to objectively true statements about the world. Suppose someone says: "I've got Archimedes' lever right here; with it I can decide objectively between x and y. And y, my position, comes out on top." The opponent can reply: "How do you know that that is Archimedes' lever? Actually, you are quite mistaken. *I* have Archimedes' lever, and it differs from yours. Not only does it show that your position is wrong; it also shows that your so-called Archimedes' lever is wrong." Such situations are common: men do not all accept the same standards, and individual men accept different standards at different times of their lives. Standards vary, often sharply, from brother to brother, man to man, village to village, nation to nation, historical period to historical period. Many men, in fact, think they possess Archimedes' lever.

Obviously, a man cannot, without arguing in a circle, justify the rationality of his standard of rationality by appealing to that standard. Yet, if he holds certain beliefs—for example the standard itself—to be immune from the demand for rational justification and from the question "How do you know?" he can be said to hold them irrationally or dogmatically. And, so it is claimed, argument among men about the radically different beliefs they hold in this way is pointless. For rational argument consists in mutual criticism, with each man supporting all his beliefs with good reasons. The limits of rational argument within any particular way of life, then, seem to be defined by reference to that object or belief in respect to which commitment is made or imposed, in respect to which argument is called to a halt.

If this picture of rational argument and its limits is accepted, the two consequences stated above seem to follow immediately. First, a man may choose without justification the set of standards, or the Archimedes' lever, he pleases. The "truth" of his beliefs is then ultimately rooted not in their self-evidence or in their universality but in his whim, or in his belief, say, that God has commanded him to accept these standards. A man's standards are *true for him* because of his subjective commitment to them. Again, if everyone must make an irrational commitment at some point, then no one can be criticized simply because he has done so. "Error" in these important matters is only a matter of submission to a different authority.

To test whether the *tu quoque* is unanswerable we might select several competing ways of life and probe them to determine whether in the last resort any choice between them is arbitrary. Before we can make such a test, we must decide which ways of life to compare. There appears, at least at first, to be little guidance for the selection; on the assumption that the following are mutually exclusive, we might as well contrast Buddhism and Christianity; or asceticism and hedonism; or (as the Christian philosopher H. A. Hodges, for instance, has done)[4] Marxism, positivism, and "metaphysical Christianity."

However, since comparisons of such ways of life miss

[4] H. A. Hodges: *Languages, Standpoints and Attitudes* (London: Oxford University Press; 1953).

the point of the difficulty, a further consideration of the original problem may provide a clue to help guide us in our selection. First, the problem concerns the *limits of rationality* in the making of a decision about a way of life. Second, one of the most influential contemporary ways of life is that of the *rationalist*, a position that might be described loosely for the time being as one whose supporters are eager to make *all* their decisions—moral, scientific, or otherwise—rationally, on rational grounds, or with good reasons. Therefore, we might turn the problem on itself as it were, strike a deeper level, and perhaps even solve it, *by asking what the limits of rationality are when it comes to making a decision between the rationalist way of life and some other way of life.* Must the rationalist also begin with an irrational commitment?

Although almost any way of life would do as a contrast to rationalism, the fact that here we are primarily interested in the Protestant tradition may enable us to sharpen our intellectual knives still further. For Protestantism, by contrast to many other ways of life, such as Nazism or the beatnik life, has from its inception been intimately associated with reason.

To the theologians we have discussed, the answer to the question has seemed clear: the choice between rationalism and Protestantism has indeed appeared to be just as arbitrarily irrational as any other.[5] It was distinguished only, if at all, by the apparent blindness of would-be rationalists,

---

[5] See H. R. Niebuhr: *Christ and Culture*, p. 252; and Reinhold Niebuhr: "Reply to Interpretation and Criticism," in *Reinhold Niebuhr: His Religious, Social and Political Thought* (New York: The Macmillan Co.; 1956), p. 450.

who rarely would admit to being really irrationalists. When the conscious irrationalist talks of the "Leap of Faith," he sincerely believes he is referring to a universal human condition. Moreover, since we all value self-consciousness, he contends that a man who makes such a choice self-consciously is not only no more irrational than anyone else; he is a superior being—superior to the mass of men who never even know they have standards, far superior to the blind "bourgeois" rationalist liberal who believes his own beliefs to be objective. More extreme irrationalists have gone so far as to suggest that almost *any* deliberate commitment is better than a liberalism which is, they say, typically unaware of its commitments. The soul-impoverished rationalist or liberal, not realizing that he cannot avoid making an irrational commitment, makes one blindly without knowing what he is doing. The irrationalist, on the other hand, is *free*. Recognizing that his commitments are *necessarily arbitrary*, he becomes free to *choose* them and to be true to himself in his choice. The rationalist, in trying—hopelessly—to ensure that all his beliefs are determined by objective standards, merely succeeds in ensuring that none of his beliefs is "truly his own."

To use the terminology of some existentialist proponents of the argument, it is in his self-conscious deliberate selection of the kind of world in which he is going to live, or of the way of life he is going to lead, that a man achieves *authentic* human existence.[6] The theologian makes an ir-

---

[6] However, existentialists are no more agreed about the importance of deliberate choice than they are about many other issues. In particular, Protestant existentialists often deny that this is a matter of pick and choose, stressing that *we are chosen* in the sense that God decides who shall "choose" Christian presuppositions. But there is greater agreement on a

rational commitment to Christ; he admits it—he glories in it. But the rationalist has made an equally irrational commitment to reason—despite his insolent claim to "hold no dogma sacrosanct." [7] The theologian, it appears, is intellectually more honest—indeed, even more rational —than the rationalist. If even the most radical rationalist must hold some of his beliefs immune from criticism, the theologian can write in good conscience, as Brunner did in his book *The Mediator:*

> Faith may indeed be combined with criticism of the biblical tradition about the life of Jesus, perhaps even with a very radical form of criticism, but it is not possible to combine faith with *every* kind of criticism; for instance, it cannot be combined with the kind of criticism which denies the existence of Jesus altogether. . . .

2 · How Shoes Can Be Danced Into Holes

> JUDGE not, that ye be not judged. For with what judgment ye judge, ye shall be judged; and with what measure ye mete, it shall be measured unto you. And why beholdest thou the mote that is in my brother's eye, but considerest not the beam that is in thy own eye? Or how wilt thou say to thy brother, Let me cast out the mote out of thine eye; and lo, the beam is in thine own eye? Thou hypocrite, cast out first the beam out of thine own eye . . .
>
> MATTHEW 7:1–5

If correct, the argument about the limits of rationality can then provide a Protestant with a rational excuse for

---

more important point: the identification of the *worth* and the *validity* of a commitment with its *source*, whether that source be a "self-conscious decision" or "God."

[7] See Dancey: "In Defense of Liberalism," op. cit.

his irrational commitment to Christ and a secure refuge from any criticism of this commitment. The theologian can reply *"tu quoque"* to his critic, and remind him that people whose own rationality is limited should not admonish others for admitting that the limitation exists; that people who live in glass houses should not throw stones.

Fair as the retort seems, and even if the argument is valid, its use involves some serious disadvantages. One of these concerns the practical matter of settling disputes in social life. A typical rationalist might say that there are two principal means of settling disputes among people with basically differing outlooks: (1) argument, and (2) force or appeal to irrational authority. And a rationalist, he would add at once, is one like himself who prefers the first course. Yet typically, such a rationalist is unable to escape the dilemma of ultimate commitment; and thus is unable to defeat the great excuse of proponents of force and irrationalism: since, for certain logical reasons, argument is severely restricted, force—possibly violent—*must* be employed when a decision is necessary. As the American pragmatist and Supreme Court Justice, the late Oliver Wendell Holmes, Jr., put it, "the ultimate ratio is force." That is, if it is *futile* to try to *argue* a person with different commitments into one's own position rationally, then one must—if a decision must be reached—resort to irrational persuasion or force. If disputes that must be settled cannot in principle be settled by argument, then they must in practice be settled by force.

Another rather ironic consequence of using the *tu quoque* is rarely noticed. To the extent that anyone employing it strengthens his own position by insuring that it is parallel to his opponent's, to that extent he increases the invulnerability of the *opponent* to criticism.[8] For the opponent, if criticized, may also use the *tu quoque*. Those who gain a refuge of safety for themselves through appeal to the limits of rationality thereby provide a similar refuge for all others whose commitments differ from theirs. Thus, the many criticisms which the Protestant theologians have leveled at rationalism and liberalism become as pointless as those the liberals have directed at theology. Ultimately, the use of the *tu quoque* makes nonsense of the idea of the historical development and change of ideas in the face of criticism.

Among those who have employed the argument of the limits of rationality to defend their own commitments from criticism, there are two kinds of writers who, ignoring such disadvantages, have continued to criticize the commitments of others. The first kind consists of those who simply have not seen the point, who have not appreciated that this "defense" forces them to abandon the practice of criticism. The second kind consists of those who do seem to see the point but who go on criticizing all the same. I shall cite two examples of the latter type to illustrate some of the pitfalls involved.

The first is Professor Herbert Butterfield of Cambridge University, an excellent and rightly renowned historian. In his book *The Whig Interpretation of History* and in

---

[8] One of the few philosophers who seems fully to have appreciated this point, although he has applied it critically only to contemporary linguistic philosophy, is Ernest Gellner. See *Words and Things* (London: Victor Gollancz; 1959), Chap. VIII.

many essays,[9] Butterfield has stated that the task of the historian is simply to report the facts, not to criticize morally, not to praise or blame men of other times. Himself a nonconformist Protestant Christian, Butterfield urges the historian to embrace the precepts: "Judge not (that ye be not judged)" and "To know all is to forgive all." The task of the historian, he argues, is that of the detective, not of the judge or advocate. Ultimately, Butterfield suggests, the only moralizing one can allow oneself is moralizing about oneself.

Butterfield fits easily into our picture of the relativist: he allows that a man may make his own moral decisions and commitments but forbids criticism of others for differing moral stances. At the same time, there is in his approach a highly misleading air of "objectivity" which needs to be pointed out. Butterfield is not simply saying that the historian should avoid moralizing and misleading value-charged words and emphases in his descriptive narrative; nor is Butterfield simply enjoining the historian not to slant his narrative in favor of the faction he personally prefers. Among Western historians, there is little serious controversy about such matters.

Butterfield's claim is much stronger than this. He is saying that the historian should not step into the picture to praise or condemn the men whom he is discussing, even after he has presented the facts about them as objectively as he can.

---

[9] See "Moral Judgments in History," in *History and Human Relations* (London: William Collins Sons & Co.; 1931), pp. 101–30; and *Christianity and History* (London: Collins Fontana Books; 1958), p. 85.

Though he presents his position attractively, Butterfield fails to practice what he preaches. For he has also been one of the most enthusiastic champions of the idea that historians should study the history of historical writing. His *Whig Interpretation*, his *Man on His Past*, and many of his other writings provide examples of such investigations into the history of historical writing. Now, the historians like Lord Acton whom he studies are themselves men of the past acting in the past. *Yet Butterfield, the historian of historical writing, praises those historians who do not praise or blame, and blames those historians who do.* In Butterfield's hands, the thesis that one should make no moral judgments about men of the past is itself a moral judgment on men of the past.

Untenable as this thesis is, it nonetheless plays in much of Butterfield's work the role of a powerful summons to historical responsibility and to reverence for the context and particularity of past events and men. Butterfield has simply made a mistake that is understandable and almost inevitable in a framework wherein the dilemma of ultimate commitment cannot be resolved. Moreover, he might avoid my criticism by distinguishing intellectual from moral criticism. At any rate, I certainly do not blame him for blaming other historians. But in failing to blame him for blaming others, I am not embracing his position. I abstain from blaming him for blaming historians who blame, only because I believe that the historian, Christian or not, has a right, and at times a duty, to blame and criticize the subjects of his studies.

A second illustration of what may happen when the consequences of using the *tu quoque* argument go un-

heeded may be found in the writings of Paul Tillich.[1]
Tillich might claim that all the criticisms made in the
preceding chapter are not only wrong—as they certainly
could be—but simply "meaningless." For he has said that
"all speaking about divine matters which is not done in the
state of ultimate concern [that is, in our terminology,
"commitment"] is meaningless . . . that which is meant
in the act of faith cannot be approached in any other way
than through an act of faith."[2]

The argument cuts both ways—and cuts Tillich. For
like Barth, Brunner, Niebuhr, and most of the others, he
is a thinker with one "ultimate concern" or ultimate commitment who has done a lot of critical "speaking about"
ultimate concerns he does not share. For example, he has
sharply criticized ultimate commitments to the "bitch
goddess" success, or to nationalism or totalitarianism, or
to traditional and literal religion. Yet, in terms of his
position, one would be forced to conclude that his own
remarks on these matters are, by *his* definition, "meaningless." Nor can this word be explained away as no more
than a careless lapse on Tillich's part into a kind of
"theological positivism." He has extensively elaborated and
complicated his position:

The assertion that something has sacred character is
meaningful only for the asserting faith. As a theoretical

---

[1] The criticism of Tillich presented here was stated, in preliminary form,
in my review "Dynamics of Faith and Technology of Inconoclasm," *Harvard Crimson*, March 15, 1957. I owe the inspiration that Butterfield is involved in a similar difficulty to a brilliant lecture on his views given by
Morton White at Harvard in the autumn of 1957.

[2] *Dynamics of Faith*, p. 10.

judgment claiming general validity, it is a meaningless
combination of words. . . . The outside observer can
only state that there is a correlation of faith between
the one who has faith and the sacramental object of his
faith. But he cannot deny or affirm the validity of this
correlation of faith. He can only state it as a fact. If a
Protestant observes a Catholic praying before a picture
of the Virgin, he remains observer, unable to state
whether the faith of the observed is valid or not. If he
is a Catholic he may join the observed in the same act
of faith. There is no criterion by which faith can be
judged from outside the correlation of faith.[3]

It is questionable whether the position Tillich espouses
here could even be carried out internally. On just what
basis, for instance, can one Catholic judge the validity of
the faith of another *Catholic* whom he observes praying
before the picture of the Virgin? On Tillich's own criteria
he can do no more than note that both he and the observed
person have a correlation of faith with a certain sacramental object; he cannot tell whether they both have the
same correlation. And lacking this information, how can
he judge validity? Tillich's problem is parallel to many in
subjectivist, relativist ethics. For example, what is the line
of demarcation between the inner group and the outside
observers? Tillich is here in an even more difficult position
than the average subjectivist. Not only can his outsider
not evaluate or judge the validity of another faith; he cannot even approach it meaningfully. Again, how would
Tillich reconcile his statement that "it is meaningless to

[3] Ibid., pp. 58 ff.

question the ultimacy of an ultimate concern" with his own practice of setting up criteria for ultimacy? [4]

In making the claims he does, Tillich, like Butterfield, has clearly labeled as impossible the very activity in which he himself has been engaged throughout his writings: the criticism and judgment of other commitments. So in talking about "ultimate concerns" other than his own, Tillich also fails to practice what he preaches. For he rarely stops at stating that certain "correlations of faith" exist. He goes on to evaluate them, to label many of them idolatrous, to deny many of them validity in his sense of that word: as expressive of the "ultimate which is really ultimate." Apparently Tillich believes that all men are equally faithful, but some are more faithful than others. According to the brothers Grimm, there was, once upon a time, "a King who had twelve daughters, *each more beautiful than the others.*" The name of the Grimms' fairy tale is "The Shoes That Were Danced into Holes."

Significantly, a recalcitrant Tillichian might reply to this criticism with another, different *tu quoque:* he might point out that certain rationalists, like the early Wittgenstein in his *Tractatus Logico-Philosophicus,* also made judgments that were, by their own definitions, meaningless. However, any Protestant theologian who indulges in *this tu quoque* at once sacrifices the accrued integrity that the first *tu quoque* afforded him. He had *differed* from the rationalist in not claiming for himself more than he could do: he, unlike the would-be rationalist, admitted his limitations. But as soon as Protestant theologians who embrace a

[4] Ibid., p. 46.

position that makes criticism of other commitments impossible begin to criticize other commitments, a loss of integrity occurs in Protestant thought, too.

In sum, the belief that rationality is ultimately limited, by providing an excuse for irrational commitment, enables a Protestant, or any other irrationalist, to make an irrational commitment without losing intellectual integrity. But at the same time, anyone who makes use of this excuse may not, in integrity, *criticize* the holder of a different commitment. One gains the right to be irrational at the expense of losing the right to criticize. One gains immunity from criticism for one's own commitment by making any criticism of commitments impossible.

And it is just here that the story of the stone-throwing tenant of the glass house becomes most relevant. There is a particularly modern irony in the idea of a glass house inhabited by a subjective relativist. Only one kind of glass is suitable for such a building: that ingenious modern one-way window-mirror glass which one sometimes finds fitted in zoo cages, especially in monkey houses. The world can look in at the subjectivist and watch his antics; but when the subjectivist looks outward, he sees only his own face in the mirrors that imprison him. This is an odd sort of "palace of crystal." [5] And perhaps it does afford the subjectivist a Pickwickian kind of freedom. He is at any rate free to make any face he pleases in his mirror. Since his world is his mirror image, he is free to create his world. Moreover if everyone *has* to be a subjectivist, there is a sort of consolation: nobody can look in from the outside. Everyone is alone, inside his own mirror cage, staring at

[5] See Dostoevsky: *Notes from Underground*, Part X.

his own face. No wonder the existentialists are bored. No wonder they complain of isolation, loneliness, "a little death."

3 · *Is a Rationalist Possible?*

> THE symptom that a particular branch of science or art is ripe for a change is a feeling of frustration and malaise, not necessarily caused by any acute crisis in that specific branch—which might be doing quite well in its traditional terms of reference—but by a feeling that the whole tradition is somehow out of step.
>
> ARTHUR KOESTLER [6]

The fact remains that anyone who is bored of being bored must answer the *tu quoque.* Is it really inescapable? A would-be rationalist who is convinced that it cannot be so gets little consolation from the dominant rationalist philosophies of the mid-twentieth century. Although contemporary philosophers have had their share of successes "in traditional terms of reference," the feeling of frustration and malaise to which Koestler refers is their familiar, almost companionable, bedfellow. In particular, those who have dealt with problems connected with the rationality of belief and action have often suspected, in their bewilderment, that something must be wrong with the problems of philosophy.[7] And they have gone on to wonder aloud whether relativism of the kind discussed in these pages might seem unavoidable only because something is deeply out of order in our entire philosophical tradition. But it is

[6] *The Sleepwalkers,* p. 520.

[7] For two out of hundreds of examples, see H. A. Pritchard: "Does Moral Philosophy Rest on a Mistake?" in A. I. Melden: *Ethical Theories;* and S. E. Toulmin: *The Place of Reason in Ethics* (Cambridge; Cambridge University Press; 1953), pp. 202–21.

easier to feel uneasy than to detect the error. The "discovery" of the "error" and with it the "revolution" in philosophy have in fact themselves become regular features of modern philosophy.

Generally speaking, the various revolutions in philosophy can be characterized by reference to the solution they offer to what I believe is the fundamental problem of modern philosophy. This is the problem of defeating the *tu quoque* by showing that it is possible to choose in a nonarbitrary way among competing, mutually exclusive theories, and—more broadly speaking—among competing "ways of life." This is, I believe, more fundamental than what has been called the "central problem of the theory of knowledge": namely, the demarcation of science from non-science.[8]

The broader problem became important in modern intellectual history during the Renaissance, when for the first time since antiquity men were faced with a great number of radically competing views and the need to decide among them. During the Reformation, the Counter Reformation, and the attendant scientific revolution, it explicitly became one of the main preoccupations of philosophers. And the interest in it is far older than the Renaissance. Indeed, one of the main stimulants to discussion of the problem during the immediate post-Reformation period was the translation and popularization of the writings of the ancient Pyrrhonian sceptic, Sextus Empiricus.

[8] Popper: *The Logic of Scientific Discovery*, p. 34. These two problems, as well as the different problems of demarcating rational beliefs from irrational beliefs and of demarcating true beliefs from false beliefs, have often been identified, thus causing considerable confusion, including the positivist identification of non-science and non-sense.

Behind the early modern attempts to solve this problem lay a very practical aim: namely, to show that philosophical disputes could be settled in an orderly and rational way, to show that the traditional political, intellectual, and religious authorities—which had in many cases come to seem arbitrary and irrational—could be *displaced* without intellectual chaos, *since* they would be *replaced* by the authority of reason. The various schools of philosophy arose in an attempt to adjudicate among competing views by providing *rational* authorities to substitute for unwanted forms of traditional and hereditary authority.

Practically every revolution in philosophy since then has disclosed that the previous candidate for intellectual authority was unsatisfactory and has proposed a new, supposedly more satisfactory, rational authority. The church should be replaced by intellectual intuition, intellectual intuition by sense experience, sense experience by a particular language system. And so on. These revolutions have had a depressingly similar pattern. And since, as we shall see, the pattern itself dooms the revolutions to failure, future philosophical revolutions that remain within this pattern cannot succeed. However, I propose to break the pattern by calling attention to it and showing that it is not necessary.

But just why have previous revolutions failed? And what is the structural defect, the pattern, that dooms them to failure?

First, it must be understood that these revolutions have been stages in the search for *rationalist identity*. And practically the same criticism has defeated them all—the criticism that the rationalist identity proposed by each revolution claimed to do more than it could, that it over-committed its adherents to an ideal that was impossible in principle to attain, and thus threatened them with a perpetual crisis of integrity.

Let us consider this search for identity and integrity in rationalism, and in so doing examine three possible conceptions of rationalist identity: [9]

> *comprehensive rationalism*
> *critical rationalism*
> *comprehensively critical rationalism*

The story of modern philosophy can be told to a large extent in terms of the history of comprehensive rationalism. Most contemporary philosophies are forms of critical rationalism. Yet both conceptions of rationalism share the structural defect I have mentioned. To go from critical rationalism to comprehensively critical rationalism involves a change in the *structure* of philosophical revolution. This third concept, which fuses the comprehensive aims of comprehensive rationalism with the critical spirit of critical rationalism, is my own attempt to salvage, in a dialectical way, the good intentions of the other two concepts while avoiding the attendant difficulties. That is, I shall try to reach a new conception of rationalist identity which will satisfactorily solve the problem in response to which theories of rationalist identity originally arose—while also

[9] The three categories are not intended as exhaustive. Obviously a number of historical positions would not easily fit any of them.

avoiding those aspects of previous theories that engendered
the crisis of integrity in rationalism.

Before beginning the story of comprehensive rationalism,
it is important to distinguish between the essence of being
a rationalist, or rationalist identity, and the essence of
rational belief. Just as in the Christian tradition the essence
of being a Christian, or of Christian identity, had been
traditionally subordinated to the essence of the Christian
message, so in the rationalist tradition rationalist identity
has often been subordinated to the essence of rational
belief. Criteria for distinguishing a rational from an irrational belief (or more often, a "true" belief from a "false"
belief) were set up, and the rationalist was characterized
as one who made his evaluations on the basis of these
rational criteria or authorities, and the irrationalist as one
who did not. This emphasis on the criteria for rational *belief* is suitable only for the history of comprehensive rationalism and critical rationalism. The important structural
shift to comprehensively critical rationalism involves a
change of emphasis to the problem of how to tell a genuine
from a nongenuine rationalist.

This procedure will bring into proper focus the *tu quoque*
argument, which claims to afford a rational excuse for irrationalism, and in accordance with which—even from a
rationalist point of view—the deliberate irrationalist should
be judged to be more rational than the rationalist who
denies that he is himself fundamentally an irrationalist.

Our question, in brief, is this: Is a rationalist possible?
That is, is it possible, with intellectual integrity, to claim
to be a rationalist?

4 · *The Quandaries of Comprehensive Rationalism*

> Now IN so far as this is a complete philosophical diagram
> of every ethical system, it must show the sort of authority
> on which every ethical proposition—every imperative—
> must rest.
>
> JAMES BALFOUR [1]

The most common conception of rationalist identity, comprehensive rationalism, combines two requirements. (1) A rationalist accepts any position that can be justified or established by appeal to the rational criteria or authorities; and (2) he accepts *only* those positions that can be so justified. The second requirement forces the rationalist to be able to justify rationally everything he holds. Rationalists have explicitly embraced such requirements on many occasions. T. H. Huxley, for instance, claimed that his own form of rationalism demanded "absolute faith" in the validity of the second requirement.[2]

In the stereotyped way in which it is usually told, the history of modern philosophy focuses attention on a number of basically subordinate questions that arise only if comprehensive rationalism is assumed to be possible. Among these, the most important has probably been: What is the nature of the rational authority or criterion to which a rationalist appeals to justify all his opinions? The various theories of knowledge are functions of the answers philosophers have given to this question. These answers fall into two main categories:

[1] James Balfour: "On the Idea of a Philosophy of Ethics," *Readings in Ethical Theory*, ed. Wilfred Sellars and John Hospers (New York: Appleton-Century-Crofts; 1952), p. 649.

[2] T. H. Huxley: "Agnosticism and Christianity," *Selections from the Essays of Thomas Henry Huxley* (New York: F. S. Crofts; 1948), p. 92.

(1) According to the intellectualists (or Rationalists—with a capital "R"), the rational authority lies in the intellect (or Reason). A rationalist justifies his beliefs by appealing to intellectual intuition.

(2) According to the empiricists, the rational authority lies in sense experience. An empiricist justifies his beliefs by appealing to sense observation.

The history of these answers is one of failure. In order to make clear why, I shall sketch here a few of the most important steps in the development of comprehensive rationalism.

The great French mathematician, physicist, and philosopher René Descartes is usually regarded as the father of intellectualism. Faced by a plethora of competing theories on all subjects, many of which he believed to be incorrect; horrified that many intellectual leaders of his time had adopted a sceptical relativism in order to help combat the rationalist claims of the Protestant Reformation; and struck by the need for some rational means of assessing competing theories, Descartes set out to find something which by its very nature would be impossible to doubt and by means of which the worth of other opinions might be assessed. Had Descartes been successful in his search, he would, so he thought, have provided the means to cut off the infinite regress that produces the argument about the limits of rationality—without resorting to dogmatic commitment.[3] If it were impossible in principle to ask for a justification of an adequate standard of rationality—that is,

[3] Descartes was expressly trying to do this. See his remarks about scepticism in *Discours de la Méthode*, in *Oeuvres*, ed. Adam et Tannery (Paris: Léopold Cerf; 1897–1913), Vol. VI, p. 32; and *Objectiones Septimae*, in *Oeuvres*, Vol. VII, p. 550.

if the standard were indubitable and thus self-justifying—the relativist sceptic could be stopped.

Descartes argued that a rationalist should base all his opinions on "clear and distinct" ideas presented to the intellect; of these, the famous indubitable *cogito ergo sum* was the paradigm of such a clear and distinct idea. Such ideas would not themselves need justification because to doubt them would be absurd—to doubt, indeed, the veracity of God. Like the Protestant Martin Luther, the Roman Catholic Descartes invoked God to objectify his subjective certainty. Complementing this theory of knowledge was a theory of error. Error is produced by the will, which leads men to claim to know something before they have reduced it to clear and distinct ideas.

This conception of rationalist identity began to be eroded almost at once in the seventeenth century, not only by sceptics like Gassendi and Sorbière and Aristotelians like Voetius, but even by philosophers like Leibniz who held views similar to Descartes's. In the eighteenth century, Locke and Hume advanced further strong arguments against the approach; and finally Kant radically and conclusively undermined it. There were hundreds of difficulties in intellectualism—not the least of which was that far from being indubitable our intellectual intuitions are notoriously unreliable and variable. But the basic objection to all intellectualistic varieties of comprehensive rationalism was (and is) that even if they are assumed to be indubitable themselves, *they still let in too much*; they are "too wide." As Kant showed with his "antinomies," [4] clear

---

[4] Anticipated in part, incidentally, by several other philosophers, including the American colonial theologian Jonathan Edwards. See "The Insuf-

and distinct ideas could lead to two contradictory theories. It would be impossible, therefore, on the basis of clear and distinct ideas alone, to decide rationally between such theories. The fact that one's beliefs had been deduced from clear and distinct ideas was a distinctly insufficient guarantee of their rationality.

The other main answer to the question of the nature of the rational authority was the empiricist sense experience. Modern versions of this view, stemming primarily from the work of Bacon, Locke, and Hume, culminate in such twentieth-century movements as logical positivism. According to most empiricist views, a rationalist derives all his knowledge from sense observation, stopping the infinite regress of demands for justification not with indubitable ideas of the intellect but with sense observations (sense data) which, it is suggested, are manifestly true, "incorrigible," unable to be challenged. Here it is usually nature, rather than God, who does not deceive. Whereas for Descartes an irrationalist was one who held beliefs that could not be derived from clear and distinct ideas, for the empiricist the irrationalist is one who entertains notions and theories which cannot be derived from sense observations or who holds theories with greater conviction than the sense observations warrant.

Convincing arguments against empiricism have existed since antiquity. But the attack that has had the greatest impact on modern philosophy is that of David Hume, who

---

ficiency of Reason as a Substitute for Revelation," Chap. VII of his *Miscellaneous Observations on Important Theological Subjects;* this chapter is reprinted in *The Development of American Philosophy,* ed. Muelder and Sears (Cambridge, Mass.: Houghton Mifflin Company; 1940), pp. 29–36.

in his *Treatise* and *Enquiry* gave empiricism an empiricist routing. Developing and strengthening the arguments of the ancient Pyrrhonian sceptics as recorded by Sextus Empiricus (*c.* A.D. 200)[5] and revived in the sixteenth and seventeenth centuries, Hume reluctantly came to the conclusion that inductive (or, as he thought, scientific) reasoning was an irrational procedure.

Empiricists like Hume had hoped for a rational criterion, sense experience, on whose authority it would be possible to exclude various ideas like God, demons, angels, and the like, which obviously could not be derived from sense experience and whose existence could not be proved by appealing to the intellect either. Hume's arguments, however, showed that—quite apart from the question whether sense experience, far from being indubitable, was not really rather unreliable—the empiricist criterion was inadequate; it excluded not only belief in God and the angels but also belief in scientific laws, memory, and other people. None of these could be reduced to sense experience; empiricism in effect reduced to *solipsism*—that is, to one variety of the radical subjectivism of what I have called life in the mirror cage. Since it is unconvincing to call a man irrational for believing that other people exist and have minds, empiricism also had evidently failed to provide an adequate characterization of the rationalist. Whereas the main fault of intellectualism had been to include too much, to ascribe rationality to untenable views, the main fault of empiricism was to exclude too much, to exclude obviously tenable

[5] Sextus Empiricus, translated into English by R. G. Bury (Cambridge, Mass.: Harvard University Press; 1955), 4 vols. See especially Vol. I, Book II, Chap. 4, pp. 163–5.

views as irrational. It was, therefore, too narrow for the
purpose at hand.[6]

Whereas empiricism had gained much of its influence
and support because of its claim to provide an unim-
peachable rational authority to counter tyrannical irrational
authority such as that of the Roman Catholic Church,
submission to this so-called rational authority, sense experience, became for the post-Humean empiricists an
irrational procedure too. And if scientific activity thus
rested on illogical psychological habit, who could offer a
convincing argument against a man with different habits?
As Bertrand Russell put it, more strongly, if there were
no answer to Hume's argument, there would be "no intellectual difference between sanity and insanity."[7]

In the years immediately following Hume's attack, and
indeed throughout the nineteenth century, irrationalists
taunted the empiricists about their dilemmas. However,
these blows were cushioned by the influence of Kant, who
in 1781 began to publish his bold critiques of pure and
practical reason in an attempt to synthesize intellectualism
and empiricism and to provide a place for religion, too.
This attempt—a sophisticated and complicated variety of
comprehensive rationalism—largely dominated philosophy,
and the relations between philosophy and theology, during
the nineteenth century. However, the philosophies of Kant
and his followers, such as Russell himself, whose own

[6] It was also, but less importantly, too wide, just as intellectualism was
also, less importantly, too narrow. The terms "too narrow" and "too wide"
were introduced by Popper. See his "Demarcation between Science and
Metaphysics," op. cit.

[7] *A History of Western Philosophy* (New York: Simon and Schuster;
1945), p. 673.

final attempt in *Human Knowledge: Its Scope and Limits* was Kantian, have now also broken down.

Worse, the various kinds of comprehensive rationalism today seem to be in far greater difficulties than most eighteenth-century philosophers anticipated. One of these difficulties is connected with a number of principles—such as the "law of causality" and "determinism," as well as "the principle of induction"—which for several hundred years have been regarded as part of the intellectual equipment of any rationalist, whether or not they have been interpreted as essential to his rationality. However, it now appears that these principles not only cannot be justified rationally through sense experience; more serious still, they lead to internal difficulties and inconsistencies, and in some cases patently fail even to provide solutions for the problems they were intended to solve.

Despite these formidable difficulties, comprehensive rationalism has been able to stay alive—particularly in its empiricist forms—by a number of repair measures. One important secondary reason for this tenacity is that the practical effects of the crisis of identity in rationalism have been far less serious than those of its crisis of integrity. However difficult it may be today to identify a Christian by the way he argues, it is relatively easy to spot a serious rationalist. He is typified by his fervent opposition to "woolly formulation" and pretentious pontification in philosophical matters, and his devotion to science and "the scientific attitude."

One of the medicines modern comprehensive rationalists have tried in order to immunize themselves from the complaints that brought about the death of earlier intellectualism and empiricism is particularly ingenious. To deal with the fact that many seemingly rational beliefs—like scientific laws, the principle of induction, and the belief in the existence of other minds—could not be justified by appealing to intellect or sense experience, some rationalists argued that the trouble lay in the fact that the problem of justification was stated in terms of broad concepts like "belief." Actually, they insisted, our beliefs are of many different logical types. Some of them—those which do actually say something about the world—need to be justified by appeal to, say, sense experience. But other beliefs do not *describe* but perform some other job. In pragmatist or instrumentalist varieties of comprehensive rationalism, scientific laws, memory, and other minds, along with such troublesome principles as that of determinism, become "useful instrumental beliefs." Such statements say nothing descriptive about reality, but help us get around in it. From this it follows, so it is claimed, that such things need not be justified on factual grounds (*i.e.*, derived from sense experience), but only on such grounds as their predictive or classificatory usefulness. They are in fact tools we have invented to help simplify and organize our basic sense experiences, to derive from one set of experiences the prediction of another, perhaps to engineer our activities better. Scientific activity is a sort of "glorified plumbing," but never glorified enough to "plumb the depths." Moreover, if such notions are just tools, their internal troubles hardly matter; we can use them when they are useful and discard them for other tools when they break down.[8]

[8] Yet another device to deal with the fact that scientific theories could not be derived from observational experiences was "inductive logic," an

This instrumentalist view has been very influential and seems, on the face of it, to work. But when it is probed a bit, most of the old troubles of comprehensive rationalism reappear. Like the *tu quoque* argument, instrumentalism is an ultimate weapon: once the other side learns how to use it, there is no such thing as winning or losing any more.

To begin with, irrationalists were delighted to find empiricists being forced (by the inadequacies of their view) to justify instrumentally beliefs that were empirically unjustifiable—not only grand principles like causality, but even scientific theories which, in making assertions about the hidden structure of the universe as a whole, cannot be strictly justified or verified by experience. Irrationalists could take to instrumentalism as a duck takes to water since instrumentalism removed the possibility of a clash between science and any irrational commitment. The idea of intellectual instruments or *tools*, with its overtones of carpentry and plumbing, grew into the more dignified and aesthetically appealing notion of *symbols*. God, freedom, immortality, and even angels reappeared as instruments, "heuristic fictions," and then as symbols. They too could not be proved or justified empirically; they too were full of internal conflict. But who could deny that it might be *useful* to believe in God? Who could deny that such beliefs might help simplify and organize our experience, particularly if we added "moral experience" to the sense data of the empiricists?

---

attempt to support scientific theories with "probability." These attempts have also foundered. Popper has shown that a scientific law has *zero* probability. (*Logic of Scientific Discovery, passim*); and Rudolf Carnap has agreed in his *Logical Foundations of Probability*.

The dangerous opening to irrationalism which instrumentalism allowed can be seen in some of the classic statements of the pragmatist-instrumentalist position which appear in William James's famous essays, "The Sentiment of Rationality" (1879) and "The Will to Believe" (1896); and in his book, *The Varieties of Religious Experience* (1902). The first essay contains a penetrating and largely sound polemic on some views W. K. Clifford developed in his *Ethics of Belief*, a famous nineteenth-century statement of comprehensive rationalism which is still very influential today.[9] Himself a scientist and a kind of empiricist, James demanded that philosophers honestly admit that men cannot help going beyond the evidence; that they require beliefs for which they can provide no justification in sense experience. He went on to state that men have a right to choose as they wish—that is, on "non-intellectual grounds"—whenever they have a genuine option, *i.e.* when it is impossible to avoid making a choice, and when the opinion they prefer is not ruled out either by logical grounds or sense observations.

From the pragmatist philosopher William James to neo-orthodox theologians like Tillich and Niebuhr, such arguments have not changed much basically. In some respects they have grown more refined; and terminology and details have altered. In particular, the idea of "symbol"—especially when linked with either Adlerian or Jungian psychologies —has taken on a somewhat more substantial form.[1]

[9] For example, J. Bronowski uses and endorses Clifford's views in the last section of his *Science and Human Values* (New York: Julian Messner; 1956), pp. 84 ff.

[1] Adler appropriated the instrumentalist idea of the "heuristic fiction" from Hans Vaihinger's *The Philosophy of 'As If'* (London: Routledge &

Another unintended consequence of pragmatism and instrumentalism is the opening they allow for the contention that many of the opinions men hold can be correlated with arbitrary irrational factors like environment, social class, religion, financial position, geographical location, nationality, historical period. For example, the Marxist position, according to which an ideology is the instrument or tool of an economic class, a function of the material conditions of life, links beautifully with the instrumentalist stance. Who could deny rationally that some of these commitments might not be due to the intervening action of Barth's God?

So the retreat into instrumentalism, far from resolving the crisis of integrity in rationalism, seems to have backfired, to have furthered the *irrationalist* cause. And the *tu quoque*, incidentally, crops up all over again: the decision to use one set of instruments rather than another is said to be arbitrary and subjective; so the defensive stratagems are not successful in preventing the problem from rearising.

Faced by such objections, a recalcitrant comprehensive rationalist might shrug his shoulders and admit that perhaps he had not yet put forward an adequate characterization of rationalism or a standard by which all rational beliefs could be justified and all irrational beliefs excluded. But this, he might aver, indicates no more than a temporary lack of success; eventually, comprehensive rationalism would triumph.

Any such optimism about the future of comprehensive rationalism is quite misguided. For it can be shown that

---

Kegan Paul; 1924). Tillich and Niebuhr have both been deeply influenced by Jung as well as by Freud.

comprehensive rationalism is unattainable *in principle*. Let us for a moment return to the two requirements for a comprehensive rationalist cited above. These are: (1) that any position which can be justified or established by rational argument is to be accepted; and (2) that *only* positions which can be justified or established by rational argument are to be accepted. The comprehensive rationalist accepts anything that can be rationally justified, and also is ready to justify rationally anything that he accepts.

Arguments undermining comprehensive rationalism existed long before Descartes, let alone the empiricists, composed his theories. But it took the practical breakdown of intellectualist and empiricist forms of comprehensive rationalism to bring home to most philosophers the fact that arguments showing that their position was theoretically impossible were not simply intellectual cheats.

There are many ways to demonstrate that comprehensive rationalism is not attainable. I shall begin by showing that the two requirements cannot be held simultaneously: if we take the second requirement seriously, then we must try to justify the first requirement. But this cannot be done. First, the requirement is not in fact justifiable by sense experience, by intellectual intuition of clear and distinct ideas, or by any other rational authority ever proposed. Second, any such justification of the practice of accepting the results of argument, even if it could *per impossibile* be carried out, would be pointless unless it were already accepted that a justification should be accepted at least here —which is just what is in part at issue. The argument would be generally convincing only to those persons who had *already adopted* the belief that arguments should count. To put the point in a stronger form: it is pointless to try to prove something to a person who does not accept that proofs should be accepted.[2] So it is in fact impossible to quell doubts about the principle by justifying it through argument. It seems that an argument in favor of this requirement, in order to be effective, would presuppose a rationalist commitment. Tillich's statement, quoted above, seems to be relevant: "That which is meant in the act of faith cannot be approached in any other way than through an act of faith."

But if the rationality of the first requirement cannot be justified either theoretically or practically through argument, then one cannot after all maintain *both* the first and second requirements. For the second requirement forbids the holding of any unjustifiable principles. On the assumption that we must then choose between the two requirements, the question becomes which to reject.

Now there are several good reasons for rejecting the second requirement rather than the first. Since we are searching for an adequate rationalist identity, we shall hardly want to abandon the demand that the rationalist accept any position that can be rationally justified. Moreover, the second requirement can be shown by argument to be self-contradictory. (To be sure, had we rejected the first requirement instead, this contradiction need not have

[2] Similar arguments are anticipated in Plato's question (See *Meno* and *Protagoras*) whether virtue can be taught; and appear fairly explicitly in Aristotle's *Nichomachean Ethics*, 1095 b., and in the work of a number of other writers, including F. H. Bradley's "Why Should I Be Moral?," published in Melden: *Ethical Theories*, pp. 346, 348. See also Melden's essay in the same volume, "On the Nature and Problems of Ethics," and Popper: *The Open Society and Its Enemies* (Princeton: Princeton University Press; 1950), p. 416.

bothered us: for if we are not obliged to accept the conclusions of argument, we are not obliged to accept that the second requirement is self-contradictory or that it should therefore be rejected.) The second requirement is self-contradictory because it too cannot itself be justified by appeal to the rational criteria or authorities. *Therefore, if it is true, it must, by its own directions, be rejected. It asserts its own untenability.*

Hence, if these arguments are sound, the second requirement is logically impossible and rationally impermissible. And since it is responsible for the comprehensive character of this theory of rationalist identity, it appears that a comprehensive rationalist not only does not *happen* to exist, but is a logical impossibility.[3]

Such a collapse of comprehensive rationalism obviously seems to strengthen the position of the subjective dogmatists, and to make the position of the rationalists who seek to escape irrational dogmatism appear even more futile. In the seventeenth century, when Protestantism claimed rational support for its views, Catholic counter reformers taunted it with similar arguments about the limits of rationality. Now that Protestantism has broken with rationalism, it has taken up these once resented weapons and turned them on its former ally. If the so-called rationalist not only cannot justify his own presuppositions rationally; if his position is basically self-contradictory, why should a

---

[3] Some of the components of my argument here are taken from Popper: *Open Society*, Chap. XXIV, p. 416 *passim*. Popper's formulation, which shows that the position, by asserting its own falsity, is self-contradictory in a way analogous to the original (strictly speaking, non-paradoxical) statement of the "liar paradox," seems to be an important improvement on previous attempts to refute comprehensive rationalism.

Protestant worry if his beliefs seem irrational and unable to be justified? He is actually better off than the rationalist, since he did not claim to be able to justify them; and thereby he at least preserves his integrity. Some men believe in reason, some in inspiration, dictators, intuition, prophets, medicine men, fortune tellers, gypsies, or the Word of God. World and man are "relativized"; [4] subjectivity is complete; relativist existentialism is the order of the day. Make a free decision; commit yourself to the oracle you like or obey the oracle that has chosen you. There are, it has seemed, many "true" ways to see the world; you needn't even "pay your money to take your choice."

While the crisis of rationalism engendered by the collapse of comprehensive rationalism remains unresolved, all would-be rationalists who are aware of their tradition will be pitched into a perpetual crisis of integrity, a perpetual *crise pyrrhonienne*.[5] For whenever a rationalist accuses another of irrationalism, the irrationalist can reply that what is impossible cannot be morally demanded, and that the sort of comprehensive rationalism which the rationalist demands is, *rationally speaking,* impossible.

As Santayana put it, in such a situation the "moment is rather ill chosen for prophesying the extinction of a deep-rooted system of religion because your own studies make it seem to you incredible; especially if you hold a theory of

---

[4] See the passage from Karl Heim in Leibrecht: op. cit., p. 194, which I used as an epigraph for this chapter. See also Heim's book *Christian Faith and Natural Science* (New York: Harper & Brothers; 1953).

[5] And to be sure, many would-be comprehensive rationalists, such as Alfred North Whitehead, capitulated to irrationalism after the disillusionment of realizing that comprehensive rationalism was impossible. See Popper: *Open Society,* Chap. XXIV.

knowledge that regards all opinions as arbitrary postulates, which it may become convenient to abandon at any moment." [6] The comprehensive rationalists deified Reason, "and all she gave . . . in return was doubt, insecurity, self-contempt, insoluble contradictions." [7]

5 · *Critical Rationalism—Its Advantages and Defects*

Although these difficulties have battered rationalists severely, they have driven comparatively few of them into outright irrationalism. Rather, rationalists have sought some way to minimize the importance of their critics' arguments while acknowledging their cogency; to make their critics' *victory* "bloodless" or even "fictitious," as A. J. Ayer puts it. After admitting that their own position contained the germs of irrationalism, they have taken businesslike steps to immunize themselves from further contagion and to prevent the disease from spreading.

A few have pushed the minimizing to extremes and dismissed the *tu quoque* argument, along with the internal difficulties of comprehensive rationalism, as sophistical cheats rooted in unserious "pseudo-problems." Others have blamed the troubles on overly abstract theory that was of little if any relevance to the more important problem of the practical limitations of rationality. Occasionally, such attitudes may be appropriate. Where the limits of rationality are at issue, however, they sponsor ostrich policies; for in this debate theory is much more important than practice.

---

[6] Santayana: *Winds of Doctrine*, p. 40.

[7] Isaiah Berlin, in his Hermon Ould Memorial Lecture, "Tolstoy and Enlightenment," as reported in *The Times Literary Supplement*, November 25, 1960, p. 759.

If a thoroughly open mind were just *practically* impossible —and few would deny that it is at least that—one might still legitimately urge people to try to keep their minds as open as possible. But if a *closed* mind is *theoretically neces-sary*, such exhortations lose their point, not to mention their persuasive force.

Here I shall be concerned not with those who dismiss the difficulties but rather with some philosophers who have been sufficiently concerned about them to attempt new theories of rationality to replace comprehensive rational-ism. One of the most interesting and important of these responses to the rationalist crisis might be called *critical rationalism*. Since adherents of this view differ widely among themselves on fundamental philosophical issues, I shall use the name merely to refer to several points on which they generally agree: (1) They concede that rationality *is* limited in the sense that some matters, like the rationalist position itself, cannot be justified by appeal to rational standards. As one of the American philosophers who has taken the problem most seriously—Professor Morton White, of Harvard University—concludes:

> There is no rock which can serve as a fulcrum on which . . . claims . . . can be weighed in some absolutely decisive way. The notion that there is such a rock is one of the great chimeras of western thought.[8]

(2) They claim that this concession is unimportant, or at least not important enough to give any consolation to irra-tionalism. (3) If challenged, they tend to ground or justify

[8] White: *Religion, Politics and the Higher Learning* (Cambridge: Har-vard University Press; 1959), p. 48.

their rationalist position in personal or social commitment to standards which are beyond challenge.

Whatever its faults, this position does possess one obvious advantage: its honesty about justification. By dropping the comprehensive claim that all legitimate positions must be rationally justifiable and by candidly admitting his supposed limitations, the critical rationalist saves himself, at least provisionally, from a crisis of integrity—from either claiming to be able to do more than he honestly can or demanding impossible performances from others. Therein lies his claim to be *critical*.

Professor Ayer is one of the more persuasive proponents of such a viewpoint. Having long ago been forced to repudiate the comprehensive rationalism of sense experience championed in his famous positivist book, *Language, Truth and Logic* (1936), Ayer presented a form of critical rationalism in 1956, in *The Problem of Knowledge*.[9]

(1) In this book Ayer, like White, states flatly that the rational justification or assessment of one's basic philosophical principles—such as the "principle of induction"—is impossible. No proof is possible "that what we regard as rational procedure really is so; that our conception of what constitutes good evidence is right." Far from being able to justify or establish these principles, the best a philosopher can do, he suggests, is to describe them.[1]

---

[9] Ayer: *Language, Truth and Logic* (New York: Dover Publications; 1946), and *The Problem of Knowledge* (Baltimore: Penguin Books; 1956).

[1] For an illustration of some of the difficulties involved in describing these so-called principles, see Nelson Goodman: *Fact, Fiction and Forecast* (Cambridge: Harvard University Press; 1955). See also Ayer's comments on such difficulties in *Problem of Knowledge*, p. 31.

(2) But Ayer does not stop here: the impossibility of justifying our rational procedures is quite unimportant, he adds; for it is quite *unnecessary* to justify them. The significance of this step for Ayer is obvious. If he can defend it, he *ipso facto* trivializes his admission that the sceptic irrationalist succeeded in showing the impossibility of any such justification. For the irrationalist's impossibility argument would draw blood from the rationalist only if the latter *needed* such a justification.

Ayer's reasons for thinking that irrationalism can be avoided despite the rational unjustifiability of his standards of rationality are quite remarkable. Such a standard, he argues:

> could be irrational only if there were a standard of rationality which it failed to meet; whereas *in fact* it goes to set the standard: arguments are judged to be rational or irrational by reference to it.[2]

Ayer explains: "When it is understood that there logically could be no court of superior jurisdiction, it hardly seems troubling that inductive reasoning should be left, as it were, to act as judge in its own cause. The sceptic's merit is that he forces us to see that this must be so." Since there can be no "proof that what we take to be good evidence really is so," then "it is not sensible to demand one. The sceptic's problems are insoluble because they are fictitious." [3]

(3) Ayer has said rather little about how an unjustifiable rationalist position might be defended against critics who simply do not "understand" that "there logically could be

[2] *The Problem of Knowledge*, p. 75. My italics.
[3] Ibid., p. 81.

no court of superior jurisdiction" beyond certain standards whose rationality they do not *in fact* accept. On this point Professor White has been somewhat more explicit. In the course of discussing and endorsing Ayer's position, and pointing up its many similarities to recent forms of logical pragmatism in America, such as those also advocated by W. V. Quine and Nelson Goodman, White suggested that if we want to defend something like the "general practice of basing our knowledge claims on experience," then "we can do no more than appeal to the *accepted code* for the transmissibility of the right to be sure . . . to the accepted way of speaking." [4] The business of the philosophically minded person, White agrees with Ayer, is to analyse and express in principles the patterns of these accepted codes. But to test the adequacy of his analyses, the philosopher can do no more than check them "against the moral convictions which he and others share." [5] So the rationalist position, unable to be rationally based or justified, is finally based on moral commitment.

This view, I believe, is as mistaken as it is sophisticated. From a structural standpoint, the position of the arch rationalists and anti-theologians Ayer and White is almost exactly parallel to that of the arch theologian and anti-rationalist Karl Barth (as described in the previous chapter) —however radically their substantive opinions differ. Barth also argued that although the content of the Word of God might be expounded or described, it was neither possible

---

[4] White, op. cit., p. 47. My italics.

[5] Ibid., p. 8. See also White: *Toward Reunion in Philosophy*; S. E. Toulmin: *The Place of Reason in Ethics*; p. 217; and Richard Wollheim: "Without Doubt or Dogma: The Logic of Liberalism," *The Nation*, July 28, 1956.

nor necessary for the theologian to apologize for it, to defend it against sceptical criticism by trying to justify it in some way. To do so was logically impossible anyway; and it was unnecessary and irreverent for one who was already genuinely committed to it. There could be no assessment of the Word of God or of the Christian's ultimate commitment to it since the Word of God was itself the standard, measure, or criterion to which any such assessment would have to appeal.

Although the parallel drawn here may annoy some rationalists, I do not believe that it is at all unfair. Far from intending to make Ayer and White "guilty by association" with the argument of a theologian, I in fact admire in their work most of the same things I admire in Barth's: the rigor with which the viewpoint is expounded; and the candor with which its unjustifiability is admitted.

Nonetheless, Ayer and White do still beg the main question just as flagrantly as does Barth; and despite their intentions they leave themselves wide open to the *tu quoque* argument and the charge of irrationalism. Both philosophers and theologians, unable to answer the questions of the sceptics, stop defending their positions and begin to describe and expound them—to preach them.

Let us look more closely at Ayer's excuse for discounting the sceptic's argument. His own position, including his conception of scientific method, he argues, could be called irrational only if it failed to meet some standard of rationality. But *in fact*, he insists, it cannot fail to do this *since* his position *sets these standards*.

This excuse collapses at once. For Ayer's argument—just like Barth's—would be valid only *if* the standards to which he is committed are assumed to be the correct ones. *Yet that is just what is at issue.* The most important historic criticisms of Ayer's standards have been precisely *whether* they were correct; the same is true of the criticisms of Barth's standards. Traditional criticisms of positions like Ayer's have charged that there *are* standards of rationality that such positions fail to meet. It is not, as Ayer says, that the sceptic demands too much, but that Ayer claims enough to make the sceptic's queries pertinent. Before the sceptic could be rightly accused of demanding too much, Ayer would have to abandon not only the claim that his standards could be justified or "proved," but also that he had a way to escape irrationalism without needing justification. For the sceptic's basic aim has always been to show that his opponent could not escape arbitrary irrationalism. His argument that comprehensive rational proofs are impossible has been only one of his weapons—although one of especially telling force against comprehensive rationalists.

So far, my criticisms of Ayer's excuse have mentioned only the existence of radical controversy about the standards of rationality *within* the rationalist tradition and Ayer's assumption that the standards of one strand of that tradition—roughly, the strand that still believes that science proceeds by inductive inference and that such inference is rationally acceptable—are correct. But the basic conflict between rationalism and irrationalism is far broader; fundamentally, it is a matter of authority. In the broader sense, the most rational thing to do is to accept the *correct authority*—whether or not it is one recognized by those who happen at the time to be flattering themselves with the name of rationalist. Barth claims that his authority, the Word of

God, is correct; the Roman Catholic claims that it is both correct and reasonable to accept papal authority. And so on.

To claim, as Ayer does, that an opposing standard could not in fact be so since it is not part of his position is to bar radical criticism of his position in advance. The function of the critic—his "merit," as Ayer puts it—becomes restricted to helping one understand better the position one already holds; one does not *change* one's fundamental position under critical fire. To take this line, however, is only to lay down a "persuasive definition" of "rational" in terms of which one's own standards are automatically the rational ones—by definition.[6]

Faced with such a definition, a critic can only refuse to be persuaded by the prestigious title and ask: Well, if what you are doing is "being rational," is it *right* to be rational?

One who is genuinely concerned to criticize and test his standards should not, *pace* White, compare them with the "accepted code" and "the moral convictions he and others share." One should seriously explore the views of those who do *not* share these standards but who may, for all that, be able to defend their ideas, and perhaps even be right.

However this may be, can critical rationalism be formulated in a different, broader way wherein the objections made against Ayer's theory do not arise? For instance, the rationalist position might be characterized not by its com-

---

[6] This last point was made (but of course not in reference to Ayer) by Herbert Feigl in a paper published over four years before Ayer's book appeared. See "Validation and Vindication: An Analysis of the Nature and the Limits of Ethical Arguments," in *Readings in Ethical Theory*, p. 676. Although I cannot agree with Feigl's own positive solution, I think his article gives an unusually clear exposition of the problem as well as a good criticism of various proposed solutions.

mitment to some particular activity or set of standards, but—more broadly—in the simple commitment, itself impossible to justify by argument, that the results of argument are to be accepted no matter where the argument leads.[7] If radical argument about various rational standards were permitted within such a commitment, the objections raised against Ayer would not arise.

This conception of critical rationalism, although still unsatisfactory, is stronger than the former. Its strength stems from the fact that the *tu quoque* argument breaks down at one perhaps minor point when it is applied against it. That is, an unjustifiable commitment to accept the results of argument is not strictly parallel to the unjustifiable commitments existentialists, Protestant theologians, or Communists speak about.

An argument on behalf of any position—in order to be relevant and intellectually effective—presupposes in the hearer a rationalist attitude in respect to itself. Thus, an argument on behalf of rationalism (the practice of accepting the results of argument) presupposes in the hearer the agreement that the result of at least *this* argument should count. The same is true of an argument on behalf of any other position, such as Communism or one or another of

[7] The critical rationalism discussed here resembles terminologically the view discussed under the same name by Professor Popper in *The Open Society*, Chap. XXIV. In fact, however, Popper's problem is somewhat different from mine; his argument is not intended, as mine is, to defeat the rational excuse for irrational commitment, but to deal with the more radical and—to my mind—less intellectually serious forms of irrationalism that were prevalent during the war years when *The Open Society* was written. I believe Popper would largely agree with the view I call "comprehensively critical rationalism" in the next chapter, a view that I should never have been able to formulate without having had his views to guide me.

the forms of Christianity. The significance of this fact is this. Whereas an argument on behalf of Communism presupposes in the listener a rationalist attitude in respect to itself, an argument on behalf of rationalism does *not* presuppose in the listener a Communist attitude in respect to itself. What is true of Communism holds also for other popular ultimate commitments, such as those to Christ—and, indeed, for any other commitments I know about. And to the extent that his position is not precisely parallel to these, the critical rationalist might be thought to enjoy an advantage.

The explanation of this rather trivial but interesting asymmetry is probably that the rationalist position, characterized in a very broad sense as obedience to the results of argument, is logically more basic than the various other positions and ideologies. Thus, even if a commitment to argument is like the other commitments in *some* respects (in being unjustifiable, for instance), it differs from them here. Nonetheless, there remains even here the idea that the rationalist position must be justified irrationally in the subjective decision or commitment to accept argument. And this is enough to let the *tu quoque* back in. For it might be argued that the critical rationalist must subjectively decide to commit himself to a position that is logically more basic.

To be sure, a minimum remnant of subjectivism seems hardly implausible here. The idea that a rationalist is committed to rational argument appears, on the face of it, as convincing and inescapable (whatever the differences) as the idea that a Christian is committed to Christ. Yet plausible or not, this concession to irrationalism allows the dilemma of ultimate commitment to linger on unresolved, threatening rationalist identity.

V

Comprehensively
Critical Rationalism

1 · *The Pattern of Failure*

THE FAILURE of critical rationalism, like that of comprehensive rationalism, was foreordained by the structure of
the questions it emphasized and the criticism it permitted.
Any theory of rationality that is to succeed where these
have failed in resolving the dilemma of ultimate commitment must bring this hidden structure to light, break it, and
put forward an alternative. I shall attempt to do this in this
chapter. My argument revolves around two historical observations, the first of which is the following.

*The Western philosophical tradition is authoritarian in
structure, even in its most liberal forms.* This structure has
been concealed by oversimplified traditional presentations
of the rise of modern philosophy as part of a *rebellion
against authority.* In fact, modern philosophy is the story of
the rebellion of one authority against another authority, and
the clash between competing authorities. Far from repudi-
ating the appeal to authority as such, modern philosophy
has entertained only one alternative to the practice of basing opinions on traditional and perhaps *irrational* authority:
namely, that of basing them on a rational *authority.*

This may be seen by examining the main questions asked in these philosophies. Questions like: How do you know? How do you justify your beliefs? With what do you guarantee your opinions? *all beg authoritarian answers*—whether those answers be: the Bible, the leader, the social class, the nation, the fortune teller, the Word of God, the intellect, or sense experience. And Western philosophies have long been engaged in getting these supposedly infallible epistemological authorities out of trouble. Not only did they all prove fallible and questionable in themselves; even if they were assumed, *per impossibile*, to be indubitable, they still turned out to be inadequate justifications or guarantees for all the positions that the rationalist wished to hold—including the rationalist position itself.

This historical observation about the structure of Western philosophy I owe to an address by Professor Popper before the British Academy in 1960.[1] His simple observation—the sort of simple observation it requires genius to make—has an almost revelatory character that throws a very different light on the history and problems of philosophy.

Since the entire argument that follows—which calls for a fundamental change in traditional ways of thinking about these matters—depends on Popper's observation, I wish to make as clear as possible what is meant by it. Perhaps what is involved can best be illustrated in terms of the related but far more concrete case of political philosophy.

---

[1] "On the Sources of Knowledge and of Ignorance," printed in *The Proceedings of the British Academy*, 1960, and published separately in 1961 by Oxford University Press (Henriette Hertz Trust monographs). A preliminary statement of the view appeared in Popper: "On the Sources of Our Knowledge," *Indian Journal of Philosophy*, August 1959.

Among the most important questions of traditional political philosophy are: Who should rule? What is the supreme political authority? Both questions beg authoritarian answers, such as: the people, the proletariat, the king, or the dictator. This authoritarian character of traditional political philosophy—although also generally unrecognized—is one of the most important causes today of the so-called theoretical breakdown of traditional political liberalism. The liberal democratic attempt to locate political authority in the people was largely motivated by the desire to replace the irrational, arbitrary, and often absentee rule of traditional monarchs by a rational authority. Political authority, it was argued, should, rationally speaking, stem from the people because, among other reasons, they would know their own needs best. However, as Walter Lippmann and others have argued, illustrating their cases with examples from recent history, a populace can also become an arbitrary and irrational political authority. Political affairs might in certain situations become so complex, for instance, that the average man would not in fact be able to judge his own best interests. A ballot-box majority in such a situation might be as irrational an authority as the most arbitrary king. So democratic liberalism, by tying itself to *traditional* forms of democracy, is in danger of embracing *irrationalism* despite its intentions.

The practical problems involved in such situations are far from easy to solve. Nevertheless, the *theoretical* difficulties that have troubled Lippmann and others so much may be escaped with remarkable ease by recognizing the authoritarian character of the traditional questions and simply *changing the political question* from: Who should rule? to: How can we best arrange our political institutions so as to get rid of bad rulers when they appear, or at least restrict the amount of harm they can do? [2]

This seemingly minor change in the political question is enough to topple the authoritarian structure of political philosophy. The recognition that there is *no best kind of supreme political authority for all situations,* but that *any* authority—people, king, or dictator—may turn into a bad ruler, is implicit in the question. The change is important not only because absolute power corrupts absolutely. The ruler may simply become tired and old and lose touch with the realities that should govern the discharge of his responsibilities. Or he may, with the best of motives, become attached to an idea or ideology that thwarts his own intentions while also defeating the best interests of those he is charged with governing.

Even with this change in the traditional political question, practical political answers will not be easy to achieve. Imagination and dedication are required if men are to devise governmental institutions containing built-in mechanisms of self-criticism which will work efficiently in concrete geopolitical and economic contexts. But formulating the problem in this way reopens the door to a *rational* approach and enables a liberal to be a political rationalist and a kind of democrat without committing him to the belief that any majority is right. And it helps explain why apparently undemocratic institutions might perhaps be unavoidable, at least at first, in some of the newborn republics of Asia and Africa. If the ballot box itself is not an effective mechanism for eliminating bad leadership in these coun-

[2] Popper: *The Open Society,* Chap. VII.

tries, even the ballot box may have to be subjected to institutional checks—which are themselves, in turn, open to
check.

In his memoirs, Charles de Gaulle has described the
traditional concept of sovereignty or authority as well as
anyone: "a last resort designated in advance." It is hardly
necessary to add that he was referring to himself. What is
challenged by the proposed change of question is the whole
idea that political institutions of the last resort need to be
designated in advance. For conditions may change, and a
good last resort in one situation may be disastrous in another. The ballot box, the national assembly, or the general
who lives in the country, each may prove a good locus for
political authority, and each may conceivably become
tyrannical or ineffectual. The problem, then, should not be
how to designate in advance an infallible source of political
authority, but how to take out *insurance* against the wreck
of whatever flagship happens at a particular time to be
handling the navigation for the fleet of state. A country that
happens to possess a brilliant and humane, if rusticated,
general, who is willing and able to assume leadership when
needed, has a potentially valuable piece of insurance as well
as a potentially dangerous explosive. But a state whose institutions are so broken down that she must rely on such
chance occurrence is poorly insured indeed. Perhaps both
considerations apply to the Fourth Republic; it was "the
fortune of France," as de Gaulle might put it, that the one
happened, at one point in her history, to balance the other.

What holds true for political philosophy applies perhaps
even more significantly to philosophy in general. All pro-

posed intellectual authorities have turned out to be both
intrinsically fallible and epistemologically insufficient. Infallible sources of knowledge and intellectual authority appear to be as unavailable as infallible political authorities.
Yet those who readily admit the unreliability of political
leaders often retain their hope for and trust in manifestly
unworkable intellectual authorities. Perhaps the two are
connected, so that political instability encourages uncritical
escapist faith in intellectual systems within which chaos can
more easily be concealed.

2 · A Nonjustificational Approach

The authoritarian structuring of philosophy's fundamental epistemological questions could be remedied, Popper
suggested, by making a shift comparable to the one he had
suggested for political philosophy. He argued, in effect,
that the traditional search for justification should be replaced by a search for criticism, a philosophical program
for counteracting intellectual rather than political error.

The philosophical questions that would have to be asked
within such a program would show a striking structural
change. The traditional demand for justification—the
"How do you know?" question—would not legitimately
arise. And if it arose in fact, the philosopher would have to
reply: "I *do not know*; I have no guarantees."

If he wanted to be a little more precise, he might
elaborate: "Some of the beliefs I hold may in fact be true;
but since there are no guarantees or criteria of truth, no
ways of definitely deciding, I can never know for sure
whether what I believe to be true is in fact so." For such a
philosopher, a different question would become important:

How can our intellectual life and institutions be arranged so as to expose our beliefs, conjectures, policies, positions, sources of ideas, traditions, and the like—whether or not they are justifiable—to maximum criticism, in order to counteract and eliminate as much intellectual error as possible? This concern could hardly clash more sharply with that of the traditional rationalist for whom the main intellectual offense was to hold an unjustifiable belief.

I believe that the shift from authoritative justification to criticism is a genuine innovation in philosophy whose importance cannot be overemphasized. Nonetheless, it might be objected immediately that there is no real shift or clash here; that the idea of criticizing competing views rationally, far from being novel, has been the main theme of modern philosophy from its outset—as I myself have stressed in the previous chapter. In this case, my so-called shift from justification to criticism would seem to be just another refrain of the song: "You must be critical," which has been in the philosophical litany from the pre-Socratics to Socrates himself, through Descartes and Kant, to Nietzsche, to the latest enthusiastic student of philosophy. Almost everybody is in favor of the critical attitude these days; it has become a rather old story. And one grows bored of paeans to criticism, however eloquent and right-minded, which never grapple with a belief that is so widespread it is taken quite uncritically for granted: that there is a fundamental theoretical limit to the role of criticism and, *ipso facto*, of rationality—as illustrated by the dilemma of ultimate commitment.

So, until the dilemma of ultimate commitment is resolved, this hypothetical objection might continue, stress on the importance of criticism does no good; for this dilemma makes it futile for one philosopher to accuse another of being uncritical. The defendant usually can, and often does, reply that his is the point at which the limit to criticism should be drawn and that his accuser is himself uncritical in forgetting that he, too, limits its role.

Although this objection is invalid, it should be taken very seriously in order to bring out as clearly as possible the difference between the theory of criticism advocated here and other critical philosophies.

I believe that this can be done in a straightforward way by asking for an explanation of Popper's observation: Why has an authoritarian structure been retained—and even gone unnoticed—in modern philosophies that have been intentionally anti-authoritarian and critical in spirit? Has it perhaps been retained because it is inescapable?

These questions can be answered by a further historical observation, which supplements Popper's and makes its significance clear. Namely, the task of solving the problems of rational critical arbitration among competing positions has been frustrated from the start by the fact that *in almost all traditional and modern philosophies—those that called themselves critical as well as those that did not—the idea of criticism has been fused with the idea of justification.* And demands for justification are of course satisfied by the appeal to authority, which produces the dilemma of ultimate commitment. As a group, the philosophies in which this fusion of justification and criticism occurs may be called *justificational philosophies of criticism.*

The purpose of the view proposed here is to escape this dilemma—and perhaps help make future hymns to the critical attitude worthwhile—by explicitly eliminating the notion of justification from the notion of criticism, and by aiming not simply to encourage criticism and objection but to do so within the framework of a *nonjustificational philosophy of criticism*. In this lies the difference between the view advocated here and many other critical philosophies.

But what does it mean to talk of the fusion of justification and criticism? They have been fused in a number of different ways. One way, which is historically probably the most important, is dominant in most kinds of comprehensive rationalism. On this view, the way to criticize a view is to see whether it can be logically derived from—i.e., "justified by"—the rational criterion or authority. On an empiricist view, such as Hume's, for instance, the strongest criticism of any particular theory was that it could not be justified or established properly—in his case by an appeal to sense experience. If one examines Hume's philosophical writings, one finds him making fairly consistent use of the following basic strategy of criticism: He takes one idea after another—the idea of God, of the soul, of memory, of other minds—and asks whether it can be justified by being derived from sense experience, which he regards as man's only source of knowledge, or rational authority. If it can be justified as required, he accepts it; and if it cannot, he either rejects it or implies that at least from a rational point of view it *should* be rejected.

Descartes's method "for conducting the reason well and for searching for truth in the sciences, however different in other respects, is closely parallel to Hume's in this. Descartes's program of reductive analysis is a form of justificational criticism and his program of synthesis is a particular form of justification. Ideas that cannot be reduced to clear and distinct ideas, and thus rationally justified, Descartes thinks should be rejected—just as everything that is to be accepted must be so justified. For both philosophers, the rational way to criticize an idea is to see whether or not it can be rationally justified.

Another strategy of criticism which is quite popular, although both weaker in its demands and more difficult to apply than the first, also fuses justification and criticism. It is weaker than the first strategy because it employs a kind of "elastic clause" similar to that in the United States Constitution. What matters is not whether a belief can be derived from the rational authority but whether it *conflicts* with it. In other words, it is not irrational to hold a belief that cannot be derived from—i.e., justified by—the rational authority unless its contrary *can* be derived from the rational authority.

This strategy has been adopted not only in various intellectualist, empiricist, and pragmatist epistemologies, but also in many religious theories of authority. For instance, few theories that grant the Bible pre-eminence as an authoritative source of truth require that the faithful repudiate any belief that lacks Biblical sanction. Beliefs not specifically endorsed or implied by the Bible—such as Newtonian theory—may be held for other reasons provided they do not conflict with views that do enjoy Biblical justification. The Roman Catholic Church has adopted one variant of this strategy: the authoritative pre-eminence of the pope applies only to matters of faith and morals.

This second strategy can be varied in many quite subtle ways. Indeed, a typology of theories of authority, developed

in terms of the different possible moves consistent with the
general strategy, might illuminate some of the particular
twists taken now and then in historical controversies. Yet,
all varieties of which I know continue to fuse justification
and criticism in one way or another: to criticize a position,
one must show either that it cannot be derived from, or else
that it conflicts with, the rational authority, which is itself
not open to criticism.

When combined, the two historical observations made in
the preceding paragraphs—Popper's observation that traditional philosophy is authoritarian or justificational in structure, and my observation that these philosophies have fused
the ideas of justification and of criticism—suggest the conditions under which the dilemma of ultimate commitment
might be resolved. In fact, three precise questions may now
be posed which, if pursued in turn, lead directly to a resolution of the dilemma:

(1) Is it possible, *within* a justificational or authoritarian theory of knowledge, to resolve the dilemma of ultimate
commitment? If not, the justificational character of traditional philosophies might explain why all traditional attempts to resolve it have failed.

(2) Is an alternative nonjustificational, or nonauthoritar-
ian, approach to philosophy possible?

(3) Within a nonjustificational approach, is it possible
to resolve the dilemma of ultimate commitment? If so, how
might this be done?

Definite answers to these questions, even negative ones,
would be of considerable value. For example, negative answers to the first two questions would show rationalists that

the dilemma could not be escaped at all, and would excuse them for lapsing without further effort or complaint into some candid, if limited, form of rationalism like that of Ayer. On the other hand, positive answers to questions two and three could lead to a resolution of what I believe is the main intellectual dilemma both of theoretical philosophy and of practical moral reflection.

Previous efforts to resolve the dilemma—many of them made by men like Bertrand Russell who passionately wanted to escape intellectual and moral relativism—have not taken into account the justificational framework in which philosophy is caught. Consequently, the possibility of an alternative has not been raised and the attempts have failed.

The answer to the first question must be negative. The dilemma of ultimate commitment cannot be escaped within an authoritarian theory of knowledge. This should be abundantly clear already from the difficulties encountered by comprehensive rationalism and critical rationalism. Indeed, the only fundamental way in which the present question differs from those encountered above is in its limitation in scope to justificational philosophies—an irrelevant limitation if previous philosophies have really all been justificational. Whether that limitation can ever become relevant, or can be escaped, is the problem involved in the second question.

The answer to the second question is affirmative. An alternative nonjustificational philosophy is in fact possible.

I shall try to bring out the character of such an approach in the next two sections.[3]

3 · *Comprehensively Critical Rationalism— the* Tu Quoque *Reconsidered*

Implicit in such a nonjustificational approach are a new philosophical program and a new conception of rationalist identity. The new framework permits a rationalist to be characterized as one who holds *all* his beliefs, including his most fundamental standards and his basic philosophical position itself, open to criticism; who never cuts off an argument by resorting to faith or irrational commitment to justify some belief that has been under severe critical fire. I shall call this conception *comprehensively critical rationalism*.

The new conception of rationalist identity shares more than its comprehensive intention with the first type of rationalism. It also follows from, or is implied by, the traditional requirement. That is, a comprehensive rationalist who succeeds in justifying *all* his opinions rationally clearly does not justify any of them irrationally. Nonetheless, the two requirements are not equivalent; if they were, the traditional requirement would also be implied by the new

[3] For a further discussion of these matters, see my essays: "A Note on Barker's Discussion of Popper's Theory of Corroboration," *Philosophical Studies*, January–February 1961; "The Growth of Knowledge versus the Growth of Rationality," in *The Critical Approach*, ed. Mario Bunge (Glencoe: The Free Press; 1962); "Achilles, the Tortoise, and Explanation in Science and History," *British Journal for the Philosophy of Science*, 1962; and "What Passes Through the Relation of Logical Deducibility?", *British Journal for the Philosophy of Science*, 1962.

one—and that would mean that any refutation of the traditional requirement would destroy the new conception too. But in fact the new requirement does not imply the traditional one. It does not follow that a man who justifies none of his beliefs irrationally will justify them all rationally.

The last point indicates how much the new conception differs from both its predecessors. It differs from comprehensive rationalism in having altogether abandoned the ideal of comprehensive *rational* justification. And it also differs from critical rationalism, wherein a rationalist accepted that his position was rationally unjustifiable but went on to justify it irrationally by his personal and social moral commitment to standards and practices that were not themselves open to assessment or criticism since—as in Ayer's theory—criticism and rational justification are fused. Within a justificational approach, such a move might seem unavoidable. We cannot go on justifying our beliefs forever since the question of the correctness of the conclusion shifts back to the question of the correctness of the premises; and if the premises are never established or justified, neither is the conclusion. Since we want to justify and cannot do so *rationally*, irrational justification or commitment seems the only resort. So, if rationality lies in justification, it is severely limited by the necessity for commitment. But if rationality lies in criticism, and if we can subject everything to criticism and continued test, including the rationalist way of life itself, then rationality is unlimited. If all justification—rational as well as irrational—is really abandoned, there is indeed no need to justify irrationally a position that is rationally unjustifiable. The position may

be held rationally without needing justification at all—
*provided that it can be and is held open to criticism and
survives severe testing.*

The proviso just italicized masks a potential objection.
So the hypothetical critic with whose arguments we grappled in the previous section might be revived long enough
to make one further sally. "Suppose," he might grant, "that
you are probably right in thinking that it is *generally* possible to separate the notions of justification and criticism.
But can this separation be extended to the examination of
the rationalist position itself? The logical impossibility of
the program of comprehensive justification could be shown
quite independently of the question whether any particular
'rational standards' were justifiable. Why should the story
be different for comprehensive criticism? Would it not meet
some of the same difficulties as the former? Indeed, is it
really possible to eliminate justification entirely from criticism?"

These questions can perhaps be pinned down in the
following formulation: Under traditional conceptions of
rationalism the rationalist position itself was not rational.
The rationalist identity excluded rationalist integrity.
Under the new conception, can the consequent crisis be
resolved? Is the new rationalist position itself rational?
Does it satisfy its own requirements? Can the program of
following an argument where it leads and of holding everything open to severe criticism itself be held open to criticism and survive it? Does not a paradoxical situation arise
in regard to the criticism of the practice of argument just as
it did in regard to the justification of that practice?

Surprising as it might seem, the practice of critical argument can be criticized without paradox, contradiction, or any other logical difficulty. Just as it is possible for a democracy, through democratic processes, to commit suicide (*e.g.*, through a majority vote to abolish democracy in favor of totalitarianism), so a comprehensively critical rationalist who was not *committed* to the belief that his position was the correct one could be argued, or argue himself, out of his rationalism.

For example, someone could devastatingly refute this kind of rationalism if he were to produce an argument showing that at least some of the unjustified and unjustifiable critical standards necessarily used by a comprehensively critical rationalist were uncriticizable to boot, that here too *something* had to be accepted as uncriticizable in order to avoid circular argument and infinite regress.

Although I doubt it, such an argument may be possible. But the onus is on the irrationalist to produce it. I have, in the meantime, done what I can. After arguing that the old difficulties in rationalist identity were due to the demand for justification, and that criticism might be had without justification, I have just now gone so far as to specify what sort of argument I would accept as a refutation of my position. Thereby, I may have helped my opponents to think of ways to attack it. I try to help them even more, in my remarks on the revisability of logic in the next section, by constructing an argument against my position that is as strong as I can make it. Although I am able to refute this particular argument, I may not be able to do the same with a similar argument in the future.

Until such an argument is produced, comprehensively critical rationalism—the position or way of life which holds everything, justifiable or not, open to criticism—can be held as an approach that is *itself* open to criticism. And if rationality is located in criticizability rather than in justifiability, this position can be held rationally. This conclusion has an important, if by now obvious, consequence:

The answer to the third question is affirmative. Within the nonjustificational, comprehensively critical rationalism just outlined, the dilemma of ultimate commitment can be resolved and the *tu quoque* avoided. The case for arbitrary ultimate commitment rested entirely on the claim that rationality was so limited logically that such commitment was inescapable. As we have seen, there are no such logical limitations for rationality in the proposed nonjustificational critical approach.

Consequently, the *tu quoque* argument cannot be used at all against comprehensively critical rationalism. Theologians have argued that not only to abandon allegiance to Christ, but even to subject that allegiance to criticism, is to forsake Christianity. But for a comprehensively critical rationalist, continued subjection to criticism of his allegiance to rationality is explicitly *part* of his rationalism.

Because of these differences, the core of arbitrary relativism and of the defense of contemporary Protestant theology as well as of other forms of thought such as existentialism—the so-called rational excuse for irrational commitment—is defeated. If a comprehensively critical rationalist accuses his opponent of protecting some belief from criticism through irrational commitment to it, the opponent cannot reply this time that his rationalist critic is similarly committed. Criticism of commitments no longer boomerangs.

To avoid serious misunderstanding of this claim, and of the position proposed, several warnings should be sounded here. First, the claim that a rationalist need not commit himself even to argument is no claim that he will not or should not have strong convictions on which he is prepared to act. We can assume or be *convinced* of the truth of something without being *committed* to its truth. As conceived here, a rationalist can, while eschewing intellectual commitments, retain both the courage of his convictions and the courage to go on attacking his convictions [4]—the courage to think and to go on thinking. The word "courage" is appropriate here. The submission of one's peripheral and unimportant beliefs to criticism requires no courage, but the willingness to subject to the risks of criticism the beliefs and attitudes one values most does require it.

Second, a comprehensively critical rationalist, like other men, holds countless unexamined presuppositions and assumptions, many of which may be false. His rationality consists in his willingness to submit these to critical consideration when he discovers them or when they are pointed out to him. When one belief is subjected to criticism, many others have to be taken for granted—including those with which the criticism is being carried out. The latter are used as the basis of criticism not because they are themselves

---

[4] Nietzsche says: "A very popular error: having the courage of one's convictions; rather it is a matter of having the courage for an attack on one's convictions!" Quoted in translation from Nietzsche's *Musarionausgabe* by Walter Kaufmann, *Critique of Religion and Philosophy*, p. vii.

justified or beyond criticism, but because they are unprob-
lematical at present: we possess no criticisms of them. For
the time being these are, in that sense alone, beyond criticism. And one belief that is nearly always taken for granted
when one or another belief is being criticized is the belief
in criticism itself. But the fact that most of a man's beliefs
are beyond criticism at any one time does not mean that
any of them has to be beyond criticism all the time: this
is not so logically, and probably not even practically. Nor
does it mean that the belief in criticism itself may not come
up for critical review from time to time.

Comprehensively critical rationalism is therefore compatible with one kind of relativism. The rationality of a
belief will be relative to its success in weathering serious
criticism. And a belief that is successful in this way at one
time, and thus held rationally at that time, may be refuted
at some later time. This kind of relativism—which is due to
the fact that we are not gods, are ignorant, lack imagination,
and are pervasively fallible—is quite harmless. It is only a
way of saying that we learn through trial and error—by
making conjectures and trying to criticize them—and that
we are still learning.

Many issues of course remain. Of these, perhaps the most
important are the technological problems of what means of
criticism to adopt and how to organize these means, our
critical intellectual institutions, so as to achieve maximum
criticism. Before turning to these matters in the next section, one further possible objection needs to be noted. It has
to do not with the substance of the viewpoint I have presented but with my general method of approaching the

problem. The question is whether my theory of rationalist identity is not simply a *redefinition* of the word "rationalist"—of the suspect sort I have criticized in theology—designed to fit my desires and prejudices while avoiding philosophical difficulties.

It is not: any attempt to resolve the dilemma of ultimate commitment this way could succeed only at the expense of cheapening the whole quest for an answer and of turning a serious problem into a trivial verbal question. But just how does my view differ from these cheap solutions?

When a problem like the dilemma of ultimate commitment arises and a theory is proposed to solve it, that theory may use terms taken from language and tradition which have many different connotations, some held unconsciously. And some of those connotations may prevent the theory from adequately solving the problem. In such a case, one may sometimes be lucky enough eventually to *eliminate* a troublesome connotation in such a way that the resulting theory, while perhaps still using the same word, *does* solve the *original* problem—not a weakened version of it. What has taken place, however, is not *simply* a redefinition of a word—let alone a surreptitious redefinition. The theory *itself* has been fundamentally changed by the elimination of an assumption that had been smuggled in "inside" one of the terms it uses.

Similarly, in presenting comprehensively critical rationalism, I proposed a theory of rationality that I think can satisfactorily solve the original problem in response to which self-conscious theories of rationalist identity arose within the rationalist tradition. To do this, I explicitly separated, I believe for the first time within a theory of rationality, the notions of justification and of criticism; and I rejected the false assumption, usually held unconsciously, that these two notions *must* be bound together.

It is not difficult to see how such a program differs from some diagnostic programs in philosophy which are primarily concerned with definition of words: the "linguistic analysis" of ordinary language, for example. My aim is to unburden the idea of rationalism of excess and troublesome meanings; *not* to *explicate* its meaning and use as they occur in ordinary language but to *eliminate* from it an ordinary assumption about rationalism which prevented the solution of the problem rationalism was intended to solve.

Two of the professors of philosophy at Cambridge University during the present century—G. E. Moore and Ludwig Wittgenstein (the latter particularly in his later period) —exerted an enormous influence on contemporary philosophy with their contentions that our intractable philosophical problems often arise because special, extraordinary, *philosophical* interpretations are superimposed misleadingly on ordinary language. We then become confused about how to describe certain situations and as a result ask rather odd questions—whether, for example, we really *know* that other people have minds. Concepts are used out of their proper context and "language goes on holiday," to use Wittgenstein's apt phrase. We may eliminate such perplexity, it is claimed, by going back over the problem and tracing by example after example how certain puzzling terms, such as "knowledge" are used. We have then done all we can: we have shown how the usage of the term arose; how, in detail, it is used in varying circumstances; and in what respects the particular puzzling case before us differs from others. Thereby, we gradually "break the hold" words have on us and begin to stop stretching them.

This method doubtless has a place in philosophy. Philosophical dust-throwing caused by the misuse of language does occur—perhaps even among linguistic analysts. However, in so far as the idea of rationalism is concerned, the story is very different. Here the notions of justification and criticism are simply mixed. This is traditional and sanctioned by ordinary language, which is a great repository of tradition. Only by proposing something new, an *extraordinary* demarcation between these two notions, can the problem be solved. Ordinary, intuitive, traditional, and—so far as I can ascertain—*original* usage led philosophers into the dilemma of ultimate commitment. Thus, I have not defined a term nor engaged in linguistic analysis of meaning. If the activity I advocate must have a name, it might be "diacritical analysis." [5]

My approach also differs from Professor Tillich's "word healing." It is true that we both emphasize the importance of the process of elimination in conceptual analysis. That some men are no longer "at home" in the world but are estranged in it and from it, Tillich ascribes in part to their "looking at the world in the wrong way"—a state that might be cured by eliminating certain attitudes, assump-

[5] I owe this term to a conversation with Professor Popper. Popper believes that a number of philosophical achievements of the twentieth century which *prima facie* resemble definitions, and which perhaps have helped encourage the fad for analysis of meaning, are in fact "diacritical analyses" in the sense described here. Examples he gives are Russell's theory of descriptions and Tarski's theory of truth.

tions, prejudices, and commitments which prevent their attaining to the ecstatic communion with reality whose possibility is revealed in the "New Being" of Jesus.

But whereas in Tillich's system the elimination is akin to Restoration, mine is closer to Revolution. His conviction that Revelation happened in the Biblical events forces him to "heal" words like "faith" by amputating only the accretion of philosophical and psychological views that have become attached to them over the years but that are no longer acceptable. Such surgery is sadly insufficient: the conceptual operations demanded for the solution of philosophical problems sometimes must be directed to *vital* parts of the *original* view. That is, not all conceptual disease in philosophy is acquired; some is congenital; and in both cases some diseases are incurable. This means that philosophical theories are sometimes beyond restoration and must die.

And even if a cure is possible, new ideas and new medicine may be required in addition to surgery. There is not only disease and rebirth in philosophy; there is also conception, creation, and new birth.

4 · *Technological Considerations: What Counts as Criticism?*

Under the approach to philosophy suggested here, many technical and technological questions become central to the theory of knowledge. But I do not intend to explore these in detail now—any more than I have tried to solve in this essay the institutional problems I believe should replace much of traditional political philosophy.

The question of what critical means to use to reduce error in philosophy is, however, related to a number of current theological disputes. So I shall make some brief programmatic remarks that may help indicate where further attention might profitably be directed.[6] Popper has already focused attention brilliantly on one of the means—the check of empirical experience—in *The Logic of Scientific Discovery* and elsewhere. The problem of how to criticize, to reduce error in those of our theories, such as the metaphysical ones, which are *not* subject to empirical check has been discussed within a similar framework by Popper himself and by such philosophers as J. W. N. Watkins (political philosophy, ethics, and metaphysics), Joseph Agassi (nonempirical principles of interpretation in physics), and Imre Lakatos (mathematical conjecture).[7]

Since there is considerable disagreement about what sort of criticisms should apply against various theories, it might appear that we are on the verge of stepping right back into the dilemma of ultimate commitment. This does not happen, however; for when the abandonment of the old aim of *establishing* our views is taken seriously, it must be held that we cannot decisively refute theories either. For any

[6] This section is largely a sketch of work in progress. For background reading on these topics, see the various footnotes to the chapter, and my essay "The Growth of Knowledge versus the Growth of Rationality," in *The Critical Approach*, ed. M. Bunge (Glencoe: The Free Press; 1962).

[7] See the articles by Watkins cited above. Also see Popper: "The Aim of Science," *Ratio*, December 1957; "On the Status of Science and Metaphysics," *Ratio*, December 1958; "What is Dialectic?" *Mind*, October 1940; and his forthcoming *Postscript to the Logic of Scientific Discovery*, Chap. 1; and Agassi: "A Hegelian View of Complementarity," *British Journal for the Philosophy of Science*, May 1958; "Duhem Versus Galileo," op. cit.; and (with K. Klappholz) "Methodological Prescriptions in Economics," *Economica*, February 1959. See also Imre Lakatos: "Infinite Regress and Fallibilism in Mathematics," *Proceedings of the Aristotelian Society*, Supplementary Volume, 1962.

theory will be refuted only relative to our acceptance of critical arguments that are incompatible with it. This means that we must be willing to reopen to examination and further criticism and possible rejection all the critical arguments and critical institutions we have accepted. *But within our new approach, this presents no difficulty.* Such a willingness to hold open to revision in principle even those notions that we believe most surely to be true is part of the spirit of comprehensively critical rationalism.

All this is important with reference to theologians who claim to be in irreconcilable opposition to the presuppositions of modern rationalism. *Although theologians and rationalists appear to be in very sharp disagreement about their high-level metaphysical theories, they are in considerably closer agreement with respect to the kinds of considerations they in principle, if not always in practice, accept as proper critical institutions.* Moreover, although logic is the critical institution about which theologians differ most sharply from rationalists, I shall try to show that most theologians presuppose logic in practice *even where they deny it in principle.*

We have at least four means for eliminating error by criticizing our conjectures and speculations. These checks are listed in descending order according to their importance and to the rigor with which they may be applied.

(1) The check of *logic:* Is the theory in question consistent?

(2) The check of *sense observation:* Is the theory *empirically* refutable by some sense observation? And if it is, do we know of any refutation of it?

(3) The check of *scientific theory:* Is the theory,

whether or not in conflict with sense observation, in conflict with any scientific hypotheses?

(4) The check of the *problem*: What problem is the theory intended to solve? Does it do so successfully?

Almost all prominent Protestant theologians today accept the second consideration: they have by now abandoned those traditional theological theories that are actually contradicted by sense observation.

A smaller, yet still large, majority of theologians accept the third consideration: they are willing to abandon any theories that conflict with well-tested scientific hypotheses. The ambivalent attitude that occasionally appears here stems from the widespread acceptance of an instrumentalist view of science, and the possibility it opens for a theologian to hold a belief that contradicts a scientific *theory* without at the same time contradicting any statements about empirical observation. Moreover, since no scientific theory can ever be fully verified by experience—the best we can do is to *test* scientific hypotheses—a genuine possibility remains *forever* open, even on a realist view of scientific theories, that any particular hypothesis may be refuted by experience. Thus, when a theological statement conflicts with a scientific theory, the theological statement *could* in principle be correct.

About the fourth critical consideration—what I have called the check of the problem—there is considerable controversy among Protestant theologians, although I expect that at least a bare majority accept it, too. Those who side with Barth, however, while not denying that their Revelation helps solve human problems, claim that the Word of God, being a Revelation of God, *need not* do so: it is *thrown* at man, like a stone, not fitted on him like a suit of clothes. Those influenced more by Niebuhr and Tillich take a contrary view, arguing that the Revelation is revelatory in respect to certain permanent human problems.

I agree with the followers of Tillich in believing that ideas must be evaluated in terms of their capacity to solve problems. This is true not only of theological ideas but even of scientific theories: these, too, can be judged only by reference to a definite problem situation. Whether or not a theory is scientific, and whether or not it can be justified in some particular way, we have to ask questions of it, such as: Does it solve the problems it was intended to solve? Or does it merely shift the problem? Does it solve the problem better than competing views? Or does it create still worse difficulties? Does it contradict other philosophical theories needed for solving other problems? Is it fruitful in suggesting new problems?

At the same time I think that the followers of Barth are perfectly right in claiming that *if* one takes the original absolute *commitment* seriously, then it is at least theoretically irrelevant whether the Revelation to which one is committed solves any human problems. It is precisely because I cannot make Barth's or any other ultimate commitment that I think the problem-solving consideration important—partly as a means of bringing erroneous commitments under critical fire.

The idea of the "check of the problem" is of perhaps even greater importance for philosophy generally. Although Max Weber, Collingwood, Popper, and some other philosophers have emphasized the importance of criticizing philosophi-

cal theories by comparing them historically against the
problems they were intended to solve, the idea of the
critical effectiveness of this check has sometimes been dismissed as a vague popular notion. Now the idea of the
problem is indeed a bit vague and popular. But it is popular
to call it vague; and the unadorned charge that something
is vague is, by itself, a vague criticism. I hope to have illustrated in my own argument above the usefulness of the
critical comparison of philosophical theories against problems, and thereby to have made the notion clearer. For I
argued that comprehensive rationalism, in failing to solve
its problem, led to a crisis of integrity; that critical rationalism attained integrity at the expense of ignoring the problem; and that comprehensively critical rationalism solved
the original problem with integrity.

One reason why the notion of the problem has seemed
so vague is that most contemporary philosophies tend to de-
value the importance of the history of philosophy. To tell
which philosophical view best solves important philosophical problems it is necessary to go to the historical texts and
examine concretely what those problems were and how
they have developed and changed. Consequently, the historical study of philosophical problems is of crucial importance for even the most theoretical and analytical of philosophers.

By far the most controversial critical consideration, however, is the first: logic. Although most theologians will
compliment logic "in its proper place," many of them seem
willing, in a jam, to reject it. Usually they are far more

ready to reject logic than to deny empirical experience or even a scientific hypothesis.[8] Reinhold Niebuhr, for example, has indicated his willingness to defy logic over substantially the same issue that led William James to pragmatism and a kind of irrationalism: the problem of free will and moral responsibility. Niebuhr writes:

> The doctrine of original sin remains absurd from the standpoint of a pure rationalism, for it expresses a relation between fate and freedom which cannot be fully rationalized . . . unless the paradox be accepted as a rational understanding of the limits of rationality and as an expression of faith that a rationally irresolvable contradiction may point to a truth which logic cannot contain. . . .[9]

Niebuhr assumes that "from the standpoint of a pure rationalism" determinism is an inescapable theory and believes that it conflicts with the idea of free will and human responsibility. But he is committed by his religious views to the idea that human beings are responsible and free. Since he feels he can abandon neither free will nor determinism (although he believes the two are logically inconsistent), he relinquishes logic. His alternative course is to embrace a

[8] See Barth: *Dogmatics in Outline* (London: SCM Press; 1949), p. 15, and *Church Dogmatics*, Vol. I, Part 1, p. 8: "The very minimum postulate of freedom from contradiction is acceptable by theology only upon the very limited interpretation, by the scientific theorist upon the scarcely tolerable one, that theology will not assert an irremovability in principle of the 'contradictions' which it is bound to make good." Other theologians who seem to prefer to retain logic nonetheless treat such things as the law of noncontradiction as *categories* that are in principle revisable. See Hodgson: *For Faith and Freedom*, Vol. I, p. 50.

[9] Niebuhr: *The Nature and Destiny of Man* (New York: Charles Scribner's Sons; 1941), Vol. I, p. 278.

kind of Hegelian logic, probably the most discredited logical theory in the history of the subject.[1]

Similar views about the dispensability of logic—indeed, that the main difficulty in many of our most important intellectual and spiritual conflicts probably lies in our submission to its oppressive authority—rebound today throughout our literature of cultural diagnosis. "If a true prophet should appear," Norman Podhoretz has predicted, "his revelation would be acceptable to reason because it would illuminate life so powerfully as to compel rational assent; it would, in other words, provide a new way of understanding the world, new categories, even a new logic."[2] J. D. Salinger echoed this mood in his striking short story *Teddy*. Teddy, a precocious ten-year-old and a kind of prophet, is talking, on board ship in the mid-Atlantic, with Nicholson, an Ivy League intellectual who teaches education:

> "You're just being logical," Teddy said to him impassively.
>
> "I'm just being what?" Nicholson asked, with a little excess of politeness.
>
> "Logical. You're just giving me a regular, intelligent answer," Teddy said. "I was trying to help you. You

[1] It is no longer at all clear that there need be any contradiction here. Popper's arguments have convinced me that determinism is an untenable view. See his forthcoming *Postscript*, and his "Indeterminism in Quantum Physics and in Classical Physics, Parts I and II," *British Journal for the Philosophy of Science*, 1950; and "On the Status of Science and Metaphysics," op. cit. For an excellent explanation of why Hegelian dialectic seems so attractive to many intellectuals, see his "What is Dialectic?" op. cit.

[2] *Commentary*, March 1960, p. 276.

asked me how I get out of the finite dimensions when
I feel like it. I certainly don't use logic when I do it.
Logic's the first thing you have to get rid of."

Nicholson removed a flake of tobacco from his
tongue with his fingers.

"You know Adam?" Teddy asked him. . . . . "You
know that apple Adam ate in the Garden of Eden, referred to in the Bible?" he asked. "You know what was
in that apple? Logic. Logic and intellectual stuff. That
was all that was in it. So—this is my point—what you
have to do is vomit it up if you want to see things as
they really are. I mean if you vomit it up, then you
won't have any more trouble with blocks of wood and
stuff. You won't see everything stopping *off* all the
time. And you'll know what your arm really is, if you're
interested. Do you know what I mean? Do you follow me?"

"I follow you," Nicholson said, rather shortly.

"The trouble is," Teddy said, "most people don't
want to see things the way they are. . . ." He re-
flected. "I never saw such a bunch of apple-eaters." [3]

Prevalent as such ideas are, the attempt to reject logic at
once raises a host of problems of which many theologians,
apple-eating and otherwise, seem quite unaware. One serious difficulty is that "from a contradiction everything follows." If a contradiction is admitted into a set of views, it
will follow from that set of views, for instance, that John F.
Kennedy is identical with Nikita Khrushchev *and* that

[3] J. D. Salinger: *Nine Stories*, 1953; or, *For Esmé with Love and
Squalor* (London: Hamish Hamilton; 1953), pp. 207–8. See also Barth:
Church Dogmatics, Vol. I, Part 1, p. 8.

John F. Kennedy is not identical with Nikita Khrushchev. And any other statement, as well as *its* contrary, also follows. This sort of result inclines one to regard the logic repudiator as someone who really does not know what he is doing.

However, simply to dismiss this point of view is rash. For even the fact that "from a contradiction everything follows" is perhaps not so telling as it might seem. The logic repudiator might retort that everything follows from a contradiction only within our very inadequate logic, and that this will not happen in the "higher logic" of God or of the future "prophet." In any case, Niebuhr's claim that logic might be rejected in the face of certain considerations, in the course of rational argument, and during our search to learn more about the world and how to act in it, has to be taken seriously—if only because some contemporary logicians of the highest rank have said things that appear to support it. I have in mind the epistemological holism W. V. Quine espoused in his well-known article, "Two Dogmas of Empiricism." This position is quite influential today throughout American neo-pragmatist thinking, and has antecedents in some remarks John Dewey and C. I. Lewis have at different times made about logic. Not long ago, Morton White endorsed a position similar to Quine's in his bold book, *Toward Reunion in Philosophy*.[4]

Writing in a vein reminiscent of Aristotle's description of logic as a tool of the educated man, Quine asked that formal logic be pictured "as one phase of the activity of a hypo-

---

[4] W. V. Quine: "Two Dogmas of Empiricism," *From a Logical Point of View* (Cambridge: Harvard University Press; 1953), Chap. 2; and Morton White: *Toward Reunion in Philosophy*.

thetical individual who is also physicist, mathematician, *et al.*" [5] According to Quine, when a critical individual brings the body of his beliefs to the test of criticism, *any* part of that body may be revised and rejected in the light of unfavorable criticism. There is *no* segment of it—such as the set of "analytically true" statements, including logic —which is so insulated from such continuous criticism and revision that we could say in advance that "the mistake could not be here." Quine has vividly described his approach:

> The totality of our so-called knowledge or beliefs, from the most casual matters of geography and history to the profoundest laws of atomic physics or even of pure mathematics and logic, is a man-made fabric which impinges on experience only along the edges. Or, to change the figure, total science is like a field of force whose boundary conditions are experience. A conflict with experience at the periphery occasions readjustments in the interior of the field. Truth values have to be redistributed over some of our statements. Reëvaluation of some statements entails reëvaluation of

[5] See Quine's excellent article in *Mind*, October 1953. Compare with the passage quoted, and with other parts of his article, Aristotle's *Nichomachean Ethics* (1094 b 23), *De Partibus Animalium* (639 a 5), (639 b 7); and *Metaphysics* (1005 b 1). These passages from Aristotle are particularly relevant since Quine's article was critically directed toward "ordinary language" critics of logic like Gilbert Ryle, P. F. Strawson, and S. E. Toulmin. Acknowledging that logical language has its roots in ordinary language, Quine, like Aristotle, argues that its categories and terms are not meant to impose a false model on ordinary discourse. For another discussion of some of the issues arising here, see Popper's comments on some of Ryle's views in "Why are the Calculuses of Logic and Arithmetic Applicable to Reality?" *Proceedings of the Aristotelian Society*, Supplementary Volume, 1946.

others, because of their logical interconnections—the logical laws being in turn simply certain further statements of the system, certain further elements of the field. . . . But the total field is so underdetermined by its boundary conditions, experience, that there is much latitude of choice as to what statements to reëvaluate in the light of any single contrary experience. . . . If this view is right . . . it becomes folly to seek a boundary between synthetic statements, which hold contingently on experience, and analytic statements, *which hold come what may. Any statement can be held true come what may,* if we make drastic enough adjustments elsewhere in the system. Even a statement very close to the periphery can be held true in the face of recalcitrant experience by pleading hallucination or by amending certain statements of the kind called logical laws. *Conversely, by the same token no statement is immune to revision.* Revision even of the logical law of the excluded middle has been proposed as a means of simplifying quantum mechanics; and what difference is there in principle between such a shift and the shift whereby Kepler superseded Ptolemy, or Einstein Newton, or Darwin Aristotle? [6]

Accepting Quine's framework, White adds that not only empirical experience but also "moral experiences" can occasion us to revise the totality of our beliefs—including logic. Moreover, he thinks that those beliefs which are revisable in the light of moral feelings cannot be demarcated from those beliefs which are not revisable in the light

---

[6] "Two Dogmas," op. cit. Italics are mine.

of moral feelings. Thus the distinction between fact and value is rejected along with the distinction between analytic and synthetic.

Several things may be said about this extreme holism. In the first place, although it looks very much like the comprehensively critical rationalism I have just championed, we shall see in a moment that there are important differences.

In the second place, there are a number of senses in which logic is no doubt open to revision and in which there are "alternative logics." To take only two examples: the traditional Aristotelian logic of categorical propositions has been abandoned because it is too clumsy and restricted to enable us to formulate many of the rules of inference which are valid in our ordinary discourse, not to mention the inferences of physics and mathematics. In addition, various artificialities may have to be introduced into our logical systems in order to avoid the famous logical paradoxes of Russell, Grelling, and others.

In the third place, in order that the position Quine and White take not be seriously misunderstood, it is important to remember that both are rationalists who do not *personally* reject logic. Indeed, both seem to doubt that circumstances could ever require us to deny the logical laws. White, for example, in an explicit discussion of Niebuhr's views, has emphasized his own loyalty to logic.[7]

Still, their approach seems to open the door, even if only nonlogicians will pass through, to a Niebuhrian sentiment about logic. Because of this, the next point is quite important. Our logical theories may, to be sure, be repaired and

[7] See the new "Preface and Epilogue for 1957" in his *Social Thought in America* (Boston: Beacon Press; 1957).

revised far more than we at present expect, and it is impossible to predict when such repairs will be necessary. Whether empirical observations or moral feelings could ever occasion such legitimate revision is quite another question, and I shall not tangle with it here. *Nonetheless*, however much the various alternative systems of logical rules of inference may differ among themselves, they have one important feature in common: whenever we observe these rules and, *starting with true premises*, argue in accordance with them, *we arrive at true conclusions*. The question arises whether we can revise logic in the sense of denying that true premises need always lead, in any valid inference, to true conclusions.

As Niebuhr's conception of "dialectic" shows, he apparently does regard logic as revisable in this way. And, although Quine and White seem nowhere explicitly to have faced this question when making their remarks about the revisability of logic, certain of their comments suggest that they also regard this revision as *in principle* possible. In the following paragraphs, where I speak of the revision of logic, I shall have this second kind of revision in mind; I have no objection to the first.

The view that logic is part of our system of beliefs, which we bring to the test during critical argument and which is revisable in the light of the results of such critical argument, is untenable. For there is an *absolute difference in principle* between the replacement of logic with another "logic" and the replacement of other views, such as (to refer back to the passage quoted from Quine's "Two Dogmas") Ptolemy's with Kepler's, or Newton's with Einstein's.

The reasons for these contentions are complicated, but the basic structure of my argument is this: the "argument situation" in terms of which Quine and White (and, I think, Niebuhr, too) envisage the revisability of logic *presupposes logic*. To put this another way: we cannot regard logic as part of the set of beliefs that are put to the test in critical discussion, for the notion of testing and revising in accordance with the results of the test presupposes logic. And this is so regardless of what other critical checks one does or does not allow.

This rather abstract point can be explained as follows. The idea of *testing* and *revising* in the light of tests, or— more simply—the idea of critical argument, presupposes the notion of *deducibility*, *i.e.* the idea of the *retransmission of falsity* from conclusions to premises and, *ipso facto*, of the *transmission of truth* from premises to conclusion. That is, when the conclusion of a valid argument is discovered to be false, that falsity is retransmitted to the premises whence it must have come: at least one of these premises must be re-evaluated. If our totality of beliefs implies "x," and if, upon testing, we get the result "not x," then there is a mistake in our set of beliefs which *needs to be corrected*. However, this idea of deducibility is practically equivalent to the second minimum sense of logic previously discussed.[8]

[8] Moreover, it has been argued that from the notion of deducibility alone, the validity of most of logic, including propositional logic and the lower functional logic, may be established, without presupposition of axioms or primitive rules of inference. See Popper: "New Foundations for Logic," *Mind*, 1947; "Logic Without Assumptions," *Proceedings of the Aristotelian Society*, 1947; "Functional Logic Without Axioms or Primitive Rules of Inference," *Proceedings Koninklijke Nederlandsche Akademie van Weten-schappen*, 50, 9, 1947, p. 1214; "On the Theory of Deduction," Parts I

Hence, the idea that a set of beliefs might be brought "in closer correspondence with reality" by abandoning logic is mistaken, since the tool of logic is needed in order to argue and learn about reality—in order to bring the rest of our theories into closer correspondence with reality. Logic, then, cannot be part of the totality that is brought under test. In this consists the absolute difference in principle between the revision and correction of our nonlogical (as distinguished from illogical) beliefs, and what must amount to the rejection of logic.

An observant reader—particularly if he was struck by the apparent similarity between Quine's idea that everything is open to revision and my theory of comprehensively critical rationalism—may, or perhaps *should*, have started to wonder whether in the last few paragraphs I have not tacitly been backing out of comprehensively critical rationalism. It might seem as if I were now insisting that we are *committed* to logic.

But this is not so.

The point is that the practice of critical argument and logic are bound together. We can reject logic, but to do so is to reject the practice of argument. What we cannot do is to go on arguing critically after we have rejected the idea that true premises must, in a valid argument, lead to true conclusions. If we want to learn about, or even to describe, the world, we need to be able to derive true conclusions from true premises.

---

and II, ibid., 51, 2, 1947, pp. 173 ff., and 51, 3, 1947, pp. 322 ff; "The Trivialization of Mathematical Logic," *Proceedings 10th International Congress of Philosophy*, 1948; "Why are the Calculuses of Logic and Arithmetic Applicable to Reality?", op. cit.

To be sure, to abandon logic is to abandon rationalism as surely as to abandon Christ is to abandon Christianity. The two positions differ, however, in that the rationalist can, from his own rationalist point of view, consider and be moved by criticisms of logic and of rationalism, whereas the Christian cannot, from his own Christian point of view, consider and be moved by criticisms of his Christian commitment.[9]

I have not shown, as Descartes tried to do, that universal doubt is absurd; nor have I shown that the rationalist must hold something (namely, logic) immune to criticism. I have argued: (1) that *everything*, including the practice of arguing and revising (and using logic), is open to criticism and rejection. But (2) *as long as* we do continue to revise and criticize—as long as we have not rejected this practice —we presuppose logic, for it is entailed by the idea of revision. If we reject the practice of argument and revision we may reject logic, but we cannot reject logic so long as we continue in this practice.

Thus I have stated an absolute presupposition of argument to which we are commited not *as human beings*, because of our biology, psychology, or sociology, but *as arguers about the world*. No human being need argue about the world: therefore he need not, as a human being, be committed to logic; only as arguer about the world. In so far as the practice of critical argument is the core of the process of learning about the world, this presupposition is impor-

---

[9] See Barth: *Dogmatics in Outline*, Chap. II. "And faith is concerned with a decision *once for all* . . . . Everyone who has to contend with unbelief should be advised that he ought not to take his own unbelief too seriously. Only faith is to be taken seriously."

tant. The point also has philosophical and theological implications. Most importantly in the philosophical realm,
the absolute difference just stated makes it possible to demarcate between those beliefs that are revisable *within* the
argument situation and those that are not. Thereby it draws
a sharp line which, although not corresponding to the traditional "analytic-synthetic" dichotomy, does mark off one
portion of the class of truths traditionally known as "analytic truths" and thus refutes recent claims made by Quine,
White, and others, that *no* boundary between analytic and
synthetic truths may be drawn.

This makes it possible to introduce what might be called
a "revisability criterion"; namely, that whatever is presupposed by the argument-revisability situation is not itself
revisable *within that situation.*

Now, if we accept (1) Popper's "falsifiability criterion"
as marking off scientific from nonscientific beliefs, and
(2) the "revisability criterion" I have just proposed to demarcate those beliefs that are revisable within the argument
situation from those that are not, then (3) the spectrum of
our beliefs can be sharply divided into at least three parts.
To speak metaphorically, in a small area on the left would
be logic and in a small area on the right would be empirical
science. In between, in a much larger section, would be
some beliefs which have traditionally been called analytic
and others which have traditionally been called synthetic,
but which we can say are *neither* empirically refutable (and
hence scientific) nor presupposed by the activity of argument (that is, logic). This middle area would contain, at
least, all of metaphysics, some of mathematics, and part of
that curious class of statements such as "all brothers are

male siblings" around which much of the analytic-synthetic controversy has resolved.

The theological ramifications of these remarks can be put more simply. Most contemporary theologians, following Barth, speak in terms of continuing conjecture about the Word of God and of revision of conjecture in the face of various kinds of experience. Hence, in their basic activity they presuppose logic, even when in respect to certain specific theories they claim to abandon it. Moreover, many theologians like Tillich and Niebuhr (or Butterfield) who advance apologetic arguments against their opponents presuppose in so doing that their opponents presuppose logic, *unless* they regard these arguments as merely persuasive gimmicks. Thus, when the theologians claim to abandon logic, they are usually defying the presuppositions of their program, thwarting their own intentions.

These remarks about logic are pertinent to the more general argument because I believe that if the theologians would add logic to those critical intellectual institutions such as empirical observational experience whose value they already accept; and if they also took seriously their own claims to be self-critical, they would soon find that most of their theories are indeed untenable—that is, they will not stand up under criticism—that they raise far more difficulties than they deal with, and that most of them even ignore the most pressing problems, and that for these reasons (not because they cannot be *justified*) they are held irrationally when they are held at all. Theologians have in the past drawn their own and others' attention away from the decisive criticisms of their theories by insisting—quite rightly—that their opponents could not justify their views either. But, as we have seen, the notion of justification can be eliminated from the notion of criticism.

Whereas many philosophers have argued that we can decide as we please, freely and irrationally, between two unjustifiable theories, I suggest that we can decide freely and irrationally, as a matter of taste, only between two theories against which there exist no criticisms one is unable to defeat. This reduces the area of whim considerably: there are no important positions that can be justified in the required way, but there are few important traditional philosophical positions against which no decisive criticisms exist. Moreover, once the retreat to commitment involved in the justificational framework is no longer necessary, then it is also no longer possible to avoid facing these criticisms by citing the *tu quoque*.

VI

THE
Breakdown
of Communication

"WHERE do you come from?" said the Red Queen.
Alice explained that she had lost her way.
"I don't know what you mean by *your* way," said the
Queen, "all the ways about here belong to me—but why
did you come out here at all?" she added in a kinder tone.
"Curtsy while you're thinking what to say. It saves time."

LEWIS CARROLL

SO FAR, our discussion has focused on the historical and
philosophical ramifications of the new Protestant thought;
we have not inquired into its practical implications. If Protestant theology were, as is sometimes suggested, a subject
mainly for seminaries and theologians, the matter could perhaps rest here—the story of an interesting and understandable, if unfortunate, intellectual development. However, the
new Protestant thought and its strategy of defense have occasioned some important practical results, a few of which I
shall try to indicate in this and the following chapter. As
soon as we turn to the practical aspects, the issue of integrity within Protestantism becomes more complicated than

it was on the strictly theoretical level. The very fact that Protestant leaders were able to preserve a considerable degree of philosophical integrity seems to have afforded many of them rather easy consciences about a number of practical matters. I shall turn first to some of these results within Protestantism, then to some of the broader social repercussions.

1 · Agreement and Disagreement

An observer of contemporary Protestant life who is familiar with its history must often be struck by a kind of paradox. Whereas Protestants agree and co-operate more than ever before, they also disagree more radically than ever —and about far more fundamental issues than those which caused their predecessors to splinter into hundreds of sects.

The agreement, which is more tangible, has been given more publicity. While the old denominationalism is breaking down, the growing strength of the ecumenical movement, symbolized by the new Manhattan skyscraper headquarters of the National Council of the Churches of Christ in the U.S.A., has surpassed in promise the hopes of its founders and early supporters. The splits, schisms, divisions, and "heresies" of the eighteenth and nineteenth centuries which produced the more than two hundred and fifty registered American Protestant groups have dwindled to practical unimportance, although they have not disappeared, especially among the more fundamentalist groups. Ministers now move rather easily from one denomination to another; even where rigid formal barriers remain, clerical leapfrog is common. Several denominations also co-operate in their educational programs by planning and publishing jointly the materials needed in Sunday school classrooms. More important, new mergers are flourishing. Various Baptist, Methodist, and Presbyterian groups, which had been split not only by doctrinal schism but by the more geographical animosities of the Civil War, have been re-uniting. Two groups which differ considerably in polity and tradition, the Episcopalians and the Presbyterians, have for years been carrying on serious, although as yet unsuccessful, merger negotiations. Most remarkable, the independent covenantal Congregational Christian Churches (themselves the products of several mergers) and the Evangelical and Reformed Church (also the result of several mergers) have now merged to form the United Church of Christ. Not only have two such diverse groups united politically; they have been able to produce a broad *credo*, or statement of faith. Significantly, the negotiations and discussions that preceded the statement of this credo were often described as part of a search for a "formula."

But the new *disagreement*, if less often discussed, is no less striking. Never before, not even at the time of the Reformation, have Christians differed over such fundamental issues. Past disputes have focused on matters like evolution, the nature and number of the sacraments, the form of baptism, the organization of the clergy. Atheism was largely left to those outside the church. Today, there is disagreement within the churches over such matters as whether the traditional God exists and whether there is an afterlife.

For example, Professor Nels F. S. Ferré of Andover Newton Theological Seminary, one of the more independent contemporary theologians, has written about the "extensive

agnosticism" that characterizes young Protestants. Report-
ing that "even in our theological seminaries we can no
longer take for granted that students believe Christianity to
be true, even at the heart of its message concerning the
living God," he has observed: "Acceptance of Christianity
as a way of life, of integrity and love . . . with rejection
of the 'old doctrines,' is a common occurrence not only
among students but among laymen and a number of ministers when they dare to be honest with themselves." [1]

Ferré teaches at a moderately liberal New England seminary. W. Norman Pittenger, a liberal professor at New
York City's General Theological Seminary, an Episcopalian
school with strong high-church tendencies, seems to have
encountered a very different situation among his own students. "Anyone who knows the situation in our leading
seminaries," he writes, "can testify that authoritarianism is
gaining ground and that students want to be told." [2]

The apparent contrast between the situation at Andover
Newton and that at General could hardly be more marked.
Yet it is typical of the religious situation today that as soon
as one begins to probe beneath the surface, one loses confidence that things are quite so different. For example, if
one were to accept that the desire "to be told" may often
indicate a lack of inner conviction, Pittenger's observation
might be interpreted as indirectly corroborating Ferré's.

However this may be, another characteristic report de-
plores a situation wherein the "religiously indifferent" remain theists or "slide back into a socially acceptable belief

---

[1] Ferré: "Letter" to *The Christian Century*, July 1, 1959.
[2] Pittenger: "Wanted: A New Christian Modernism," *The Christian
Century*, April 6, 1955.

in 'God,' while the student with the deepest concern for finding out the nature of religious reality concludes that he cannot honestly make the ambiguous affirmation, God exists. . . . Those who hold these views believe that they can show that there are not good reasons for believing in the existence of God. And some of them believe that they can show that religion and the church nonetheless have an important place in the examined life." [3]

Clearly, differences that would have splintered denominations in the nineteenth century are commonplace *within the churches* today. How is this possible? If interpreted in the light of the earlier chapters, the development becomes much less surprising. These seemingly antagonistic tendencies can flourish side by side, and even stimulate one another, because of the choice made by the leading Protestant thinkers when Protestant liberalism collapsed. The most brilliant Protestant theologians, led by Karl Barth, chose a form of irrationalism that was as rational as seemed possible and also rationally excusable in terms of the problem of ultimate commitment and the limits of rationality. On the one hand, by declaring that any statement about the essence of the Christian message was to be in principle revisable, they showed a dramatic flexibility that ruled out any future fundamentalism or fixed interpretations of the Christian message. On the other hand, they sharply located the limits of this flexibility in a basic inflexibility: whatever his message might turn out to be, "assent to Jesus" was presupposed and required by all who were properly to call themselves Christians. Since what is meant by "assent

[3] Louis B. Potter, of Swarthmore College, in a letter to *The Christian Century*, July 1, 1959.

to Jesus" is itself open to extremely different interpretations, the resulting flexibility is wide indeed. At any rate,
it was wide enough—cast as a vague formula—to be written into the constitutions of the new ecumenical organizations as the key to admission to membership in them.

With such an ingenious framework at its disposal, one
might have expected Protestantism to have rejuvenated itself as common heir to the unity of a shared commitment
and the healthy stimulation of good-natured diversity. The
framework would seem to provide just what many people
have been clamoring for: a unified ideology plus free speech.
To a certain extent, the enthusiastic co-operation among
denominations does satisfy this sort of expectation. Moreover, the new Protestant thought has lent strength to institutional Protestantism in other ways. For example, it provides a powerful *explanation of failure*, past, present, and
future. Such explanations are useful in accounting for the
apparent failure of the old Protestantism: the search for
the essence of Christianity, and the constant modification
and revision of a system of belief that purported to contain
certain truth. But of course similar themes can also easily
account for the *present* failure of Protestantism: for example, the waning of its intellectual influence in modern
society.

Such an explanation is needed because the society Protestantism serves has become embarrassingly secular: not in
the sense that its practice no longer matches Protestant
Christian ideas—this it had never done—but in the sense
that its most articulate and sensitive thinking and feeling
are not Protestant. An explicitly Protestant Christian poet
or man of letters, like W. H. Auden or T. S. Eliot, has be-

come an object of special interest and attention, not only for the merits of his work but also for his religious identification.

It is true that such interest in the contemporary Christian is rarely hostile: the Christian thinker is now a phenomenon to be studied. Yet many Protestants would prefer open hostility. For although some dignity perhaps still attaches to being hated, being scrutinized can be embarrassingly debasing. The proud descendant of the Founding Fathers becomes the "native," to be photographed and questionnaired by the intellectual colonist-gone-tourist who has captured the land. As if the secular tourists were not enough, the Roman Catholic colonists, growing in numbers and influence daily, seem to threaten to take Protestantism's social prestige and place even as a religion.

The themes and defenses of the new Protestantism provide immediate explanations and justifications for this development. For example, the contention that genuine communication between two or more groups with different ultimate commitments is quite impossible is a handy notion for a group under pressure. It "explains" why one's opponents seem so lacking in "understanding," without admitting the unpleasant possibility that they might be right. The resulting argument, which may be found in almost any handbook of American Protestantism, goes something like this: These tourists do not understand us, do not adopt our way of life, our truth, because of the different ultimate presuppositions to which they are committed. It is necessary to share presuppositions in order to communicate; otherwise, our minds will never meet and we shall talk past each other forever. That so many of our contemporaries have abandoned worshipful commitment to our presuppositions in order to take up touring explains why our culture is in such a mess. Not only is one social group unable to communicate with another; even the greatest intellectuals have so specialized and narrow a view of things that they cannot understand one another. Parochialism is the inevitable result of tourism. So if our contemporaries would only come back to *our* parochialism, the old reliable highway, we would be able to understand one another again; we would be united; we would trade our confusion for strength.

In this way, the difficulties of Protestantism can be externalized and linked with the popular cry for a return to the old Protestant America.

2 · *The Breakdown of Communication*

There is then no doubt that the new Protestant thinking has been valuable in increasing co-operation among Protestants and providing an excuse for failure. However, when one turns from such immediate political and practical achievements, its success becomes less certain. For the main aims of Protestantism, as a community claiming a kind of custodianship of a religious message, are neither the political strong arm nor the convincing excuse. As a religious tradition, Protestantism hopes to provide rich saving help to individual human beings who are confused about themselves and their world, to provide an identification that, unlike other "false ultimates," does not "refute itself in experience." [4] Here, facing their most important

[4] Robert Bretall: Introduction to A *Kierkegaard Anthology* (Princeton: Princeton University Press; 1951), p. xxi.

task, the Protestant theologians have—despite quite contrary intentions—sown the seeds of their own failure: their
intentions have been drastically frustrated by the "feed-
back" of their policies. Although vast religious confusion
and loss of meaning do exist in contemporary life, theology
is as much responsible for the situation as is antitheology
or theological indifference; God-saving breeds as much confusion as does the death of a God. I wish to support this
contention in the remainder of this chapter, partly impres-
sionistically, partly by explicit argument.

In Protestant Christendom today, communication has
broken down. The beliefs and religious expectations of those
learned in theology are very often not only different from
and more complex than those of the average man in the
pew; they *contradict* them. Agreement is no longer over
beliefs but over *passwords*, which one may take literally,
symbolically, or in some other way, depending on one's
theological sophistication.

Since many clergymen are not at all eager to communicate their beliefs to the "believers," the ordinary gulf between pulpit and pew and between one parishioner and
another is widened by the new circumlocutions which make
the break with traditional Christianity seem less serious
than it is: we get different kinds of "truth," different kinds
of "belief," different kinds of "knowledge."

The resulting church services are weird pantomimes.
Kneeling before the same altar in the same service, saying the same creeds and singing the same hymns, one man
worships the God who acts literally, another worships the
God who acts metaphorically, a third worships the God

who acts symbolically, and yet another worships the God who doesn't act at all.[5]

"Well, yes," the theologian nods when pressed. "I don't believe that there is an afterlife, but the notion of an afterlife is *symbolically true*, you know."

"Yes, Virginia, there is a God." [6]

At the source of this internal breakdown of communication is the widespread tendency among Protestant thinkers today to make traditional doctrines fit new situations by redefining the words in which the doctrines are phrased. The traditional doctrines now become counters in an elaborate game. "To be a Christian" begins to resemble "to go dancing." All that is required of a couple who wish to dance is that they both know and follow the rules. They need agree about no substantial issue: neither morals, nor politics, nor art, nor science. A married couple who quarrel bitterly may *enjoy* dancing together; here is one activity in which they *can* co-operate smoothly, while leaving their disagreements unspoken.[7]

But do two such people communicate when they dance?

[5] Compare Ernest Gellner: *Words and Things*, p. 221. Citing a statement by A. M. Quinton in *The Twentieth Century*, June 1955, that "I don't decide whether a man is my co-religionist by seeing how he argues, but by whether I find him kneeling beside me at Church," Gellner comments: "*Manners makyth faith*, it appears, *and not convictions*. . . . It does not appear to have occurred to Quinton that the inability to tell a man's nominal faith from the way he *argues* is only possible in an age when nominal faith has indeed become nominal."

[6] Above I have used some sentences from my article, "I Call Myself a Protestant," *Harper's*, May 1959; reprinted in *Essays of Our Time*, ed. L. Hamalian and E. L. Volpe (New York: McGraw Hill; 1960).

[7] I am indebted to J. W. N. Watkins for the suggestion that I illustrate this point with this example.

Similarly, in the case of two Christians who agree about nothing substantial but who both know when to say the proper phrases and when and how to carry out the appropriate actions together—are they communicating? *can* they communicate? They are doubtless *co-operating*; and they may enjoy each other's company. Protestants now, like Alice, curtsy while they're thinking what to say.

Satisfactory communication with a person must involve appreciation of what *he* means when he says: "I believe in God" or "Jesus Christ is Lord." Only a theologian who accepts something like a positivist or behaviorist stipulation that meaning lies in usage can maintain that two people, because they use certain phrases in certain ways and play the game together, are really communicating. No one, of course, has direct access to another's mind. How, then, can anyone tell whether he understands what another person means? There is probably only one practicable way: he can make a guess as to the proper interpretation of the other person's behavior and conversation, ask him whether that conjecture is correct, and continue to test the conjecture against the other person's future behavior. There is no more, and probably far less, certainty here than in other matters.

Such a procedure of guessing and correcting guesses may break down in many obvious situations; for example, if the other person deliberately chooses to be evasive and indulges in answers that are intended to throw the questioner off the track. This may of course be perfectly legitimate behavior, particularly when the questioner is simply invading the other's privacy.

Another such situation arises when the language in which the guessing must be done has become so debased and ambiguous that it is impossible to know when one is *disagreeing* with the person with whom one is talking. Communication demands that both parties be able to find out in what respects they disagree: *two people cannot understand each other if they have no way of determining when they are disagreeing.*[8] But the practice of "word healing" and the "ceremonial use of language," so important to contemporary theology, have made it exceptionally difficult for contemporary Protestants to ascertain when they are disagreeing on religious questions. To the extent to which articulation of disagreement ceases to occur, any kind of communication, including religious communication, falters.

A good example of co-operation without communication is found in the history of the membership policy of the National Council of Churches. Its founders wrote the commitment to Christ into the constitution of the group with their decision that any religious body which wished to join must accept the doctrine of the divinity of Christ, the idea which is loosely expressed today in the statement that "Jesus Christ is Lord." This provides a formula for co-operation, yet—because it is itself open to endless interpretation—

[8] Some linguistic philosophers have attempted to make a point at least vaguely resembling the one just italicized, and have done so in terms of a misapplication of the notion of unfalsifiability. I believe that it is what I may call the "indeterminability of disagreement," rather than unfalsifiability, which is the crux of the matter here. See *New Essays in Philosophical Theology*, ed. A. G. N. Flew and A. MacIntyre (New York: The Macmillan Company; 1955).

allows all the flexibility that is needed for hypocrisy. One of the favorites of the National Council is Professor Tillich, an acknowledged atheist in most traditional senses of that term. Less favored are the Unitarians, who are often more conservative theologically than Tillich and who in many cases could agree to Tillich's interpretation of Christ's divinity; the Unitarians are excluded as a group from council membership. What is the difference? Tillich has provided in his systematic theology a formula and a concept of truth which enable him to say that it is true that Christ is divine. Unitarians are not producers of formulae. So, lacking the password, they lack membership too.

It is hardly surprising that ecumenical Protestant thinkers draw such odd lines around denominations, for they no longer can easily ascertain the views of their denominational fellows. When a prospective clergyman has been trained in the new theology almost anything can happen during the creedal examination many denominations require of candidates. The bishop may ask his postulant: "Do you believe in God?" (meaning "Do you believe that it is a true statement that the God of traditional theology exists?"). The candidate, who may be an atheist, or perhaps—even more fashionable in the seminaries these days—a pantheist, is often able quite legitimately to substitute a special Tillichian reinterpretation of "belief in" and reply: "Yes, I *believe in* God."

There has been verbal agreement, and the candidate is usually passed. But one wonders not only whether the candidate has been candid but also what was the point of holding the interview under such conditions in the first

place.[9] Such practices are probably less the product of will-
ful deceit than of the difficult situation in which many
contemporary clergymen find themselves. Clear communication and statement of one's theological idiosyncrasies
may involve one in awkward situations with conservative
fellow clergymen and unsophisticated members of one's
flock. So why bother to communicate if co-operation can be
achieved without it? To the personal tension and anxiety
that the educated clergyman must share with most contemporary men, he must now add the burden of playing a
double role.

Professor Wesley Shrader, of Yale University, has attributed the high incidence of nervous breakdowns among
clergy not so much to initial psychological weaknesses as
to the multiple roles the clergy are now expected to play.
His remarks about role-playing are supported by many recent reports. A former Methodist minister, J. B. Moore, has
depicted the dilemma of clergymen who cannot, "in good
conscience, play the role of good, sound, orthodox, conven-
tional, safe" Protestants; who "no longer believe in the
Gospel *as they are expected to preach it,* and no longer
believe in the denomination they are expected to support." [1] A former Congregational, now Unitarian, minister, Thomas S. Vernon, has sorrowfully described the
churchly game of "Let's pretend." The church members
confide to each other that they no longer believe the doc-

[9] Above I have used in paraphrase several lines from my review of
Kaufmann's *Critique of Religion and Philosophy* (*Commentary,* November 1958).

[1] James B. Moore: "Why Young Ministers Are Leaving the Church,"
Harper's, 1957.

trines of their church but "would not dare to let their minister know they felt that way." And the minister tells *his* confidants (when he dares to have any) that he doesn't believe the doctrines, either, but "would not dare to say so from the pulpit." [2]

3 · "A Good Atheist Is a Dead Atheist"

I shall close this chapter with a personal observation that provides a vivid illustration of both the urgency and the pathos of the unwanted breakdown of communication in Protestantism. Although I have sensed the presence of such a breakdown for many years and have often felt, in exchanging religious views with other people, that even when we seemed verbally in agreement we were "talking past each other," it was not until September 1958 that I came to appreciate how widespread the situation is even within the more solid bastions of the church. This happened at the annual conference of the Danforth Fellows, held at a camp on the shores of Lake Michigan. The theme was "Teaching as a Christian Vocation."

The Danforth Fellow program, an important undertaking of the William H. Danforth Foundation of St. Louis, has since 1951 appointed over six hundred college graduates to fellowships, pledging itself to finance, if necessary, their entire graduate programs through the Ph.D. degree. The main requirements for candidacy, apart from high academic performance, are a continuing intention to enter college

[2] See also Vernon's talk in *Monthly Newsletter*, November 1958, published by the First Congregational Church of Bay City, Michigan; and Von Ogden Vogt: *The Primacy of Worship* (Boston: Starr King Press; 1958), p. 85.

teaching and a conviction that the study of religion, and especially of the Christian tradition, is a vitally important element of a liberal education. Although the program is interfaith, and although no official church affiliation is required, over 90 per cent of the Fellows are church members and, of these, some 95 per cent are members of Christian groups.

After one of the evening meetings a group of about eight of us gathered, completely at random, in the "smokehouse." The conversation began with shoptalk, and a philosophy student mentioned how difficult it was to convey to the people back home what philosophy was really about. A second man suggested: "They usually get the idea when I tell them it's a sort of theology *with reservations.*"

"Yes, namely God!" quipped a third, and the resulting laughter provided a transition to the topic of God, which was to occupy us for the rest of the evening. Before the conversation was over, we found—to the surprise, I think, of all —that each of us was an atheist in the traditional sense of the term. We disagreed somewhat as to whether the various "philosophers' Gods" of recent invention—such as Whitehead's "ground of concreteness" or Tillich's "Being Itself" —existed or were even meaningful conceptions. But we were agreed that even if these were more than definitions, and did "exist," they were not the gods that were being worshipped by most of the people in Christian pews and certainly did not represent what Professor Ferré has called the "Living God" of traditional Christian belief.

Here was a rare instance of communication—perhaps possible at all only because we were making a sincere attempt to understand one another. Yet on the following evening the basis of our communication was well on its way to being destroyed. An eminent theologian, who was present as a conference speaker—expanding on Tillich's view that it is impossible for an atheist to exist—suggested quite seriously and sincerely this reinterpretation of the word "atheism." The atheist, he said, "is the man who despairingly commits suicide—for instance, by jumping into Lake Michigan; the theist, by contrast, struggles on in the conviction that life is worth living." In a sense, although doubtless not the exceedingly subtle sense that the speaker intended, this is a polite way of saying that a good atheist is a dead atheist.

Most of us had been swimming in Lake Michigan that afternoon, but we had returned. So we were theists after all. We could be atheists only in the undoubtedly archaic and old-fashioned sense that we denied the existence of the "Living God." Although it is probably true that most religious positions affirm life in some way, it is a doubtful contribution to religious clarity to claim that all who do so are theists.

The mood bred by this kind of unfortunately typical theological tactic was well expressed by the Methodist divinity student who turned to me after the evening vesper service, as we walked together up the sand dune. "You know," he remarked, in an idiom that would have shocked his forefathers as much as his sentiment, "I just don't know any more what the hell we're doing when we sit there and watch the sun go down."

VII

THE
"Repudiation of Otherness"

IF THE older liberalism sometimes seemed to make "what Jones will accept" the criterion for Christian truth, the newer tendency is to employ *any* device through which Jones can be persuaded to accept, for religious purposes, whatever is thought to be said in the particular heritage of the popular apologist. . . . One cannot accuse them of actual dishonesty. But one must wonder if that kind of integrity and utter honesty which should mark those who serve God with their minds is not sometimes neglected.

W. NORMAN PITTENGER [1]

1 · *Some Intended Consequences*

FOR the most part, the internal breakdown of communication in institutional Protestantism has been an accidental, unintended consequence of the new Protestant theology. Public dissension over Protestant doctrine has deliberately been discouraged in order to prevent any weakening of the various programs for co-operation. An editorial that appeared in *The Christian Century* in 1959 illustrates this attitude. After decrying the "party spirit" and "factionalism" into which "we Protestants have fallen," the editor found that public disagreement was "playing into the hands of

[1] "Wanted: A New Christian Modernism," op. cit.

Protestantism's enemies." His solution, which indicated no awareness of the importance, for communication, of articulating disagreement, was for Protestants to listen more closely to "the talk around the tables at ecumenical gatherings." [2]

Once a breakdown of communication has occurred, however, the way is open for authoritarian and even totalitarian attitudes such as flourish today in Protestantism, expressed both in policies implemented within the churches and in the policies that guide the relationship of the churches and the community. Unlike the breakdown of communication that originally bred the attitudes which made such policies possible, the policies themselves are often quite coldly calculated; for they are conscious responses to felt needs. Some sort of unity seems necessary in a religious group; yet, when the members of the group have lost the means of communicating with one another, the spiritual unity offered by the open and critical exchange of beliefs [3] disappears. If there is to be any unity, it must be achieved in some other way; and the only other available ways appear to be authoritarian, at least in temper.

The transition to authoritarian attitudes is greatly facilitated if the leaders of the group feel no responsibility to

[2] "A Protestant Believes in God," *The Christian Century*, May 20, 1959. Later (July 1, 1959, p. 782), in the Letters to the Editor, an eminent theologian challenged the editor on the grounds that a "unity of concealment" would be "insipid and false," and stated that an ecumenical organization would lose its right to support by Christians on the day it began to conceal honest differences among its participants. Several other equally distinguished Protestants, however, wrote to congratulate the editor for his stand.

[3] Watkins: "Epistemology and Politics," *Proceedings of the Aristotelian Society*, 1957–58, pp. 79–102.

rationality. Believing that the cultural turn away from Protestantism is due to wrongful abandonment of Protestant presuppositions; thinking that those presuppositions are true, that rational argument about presuppositions or ultimate commitments is impossible, that society is hence divided into a host of rationally irreconcilable groups, and that social unity under the banner of a dominant ideology is necessary, Protestant theologians have decided to advocate nonrational means and illiberal measures to propagate their presuppositions.

And when those leaders individually are ridden by bad conscience, an authoritarian attitude can quickly take hold. A man who is secure in his own faith can be more tolerant toward one who differs from him than can a man who is uneasy in his faith. The uncertain man must, like Kierkegaard, prove his faithfulness to himself by the violence of his rejection of any competing faith. Thus he represses at least partially and temporarily his dread of losing what he has—no matter how tenuously he is tied to it—lest he sink into still greater confusion.

In the first chapter, I suggested that much of the alienation and confusion of identity in our society may be due to the fact that our leading intellectual and spiritual traditions are so involved in crises of identity and integrity that those who affiliate with them can hardly do so without bad conscience and confusion. My suggestion, if correct, will help explain the phenomena of intolerant authoritarian "repudiation of otherness" which now abound in Protestantism and which are not altogether absent from various forms of rationalism, such as pragmatism.

By examining some of these phenomena, we may get a

clearer notion of how the various elements of the picture—
the intellectual uneasiness of the Protestant leaders who
know what difficulties Protestantism is in, the gap that exists between these leaders and the ordinary laity, the ab-
normal difficulties of communication, the repression of
articulate disagreement, and the plasticity of religious language—complement one another in a gestalt of deception,
partly intended and partly unintended.

Moreover, the presence of such authoritarianism in Protestantism needs to be discussed, if only because it is often
masked by a popular image of the Protestant religion as a
prototype of democratic activity. This image, reinforced
during the nineteenth-century flowering of Protestant liberalism and the proliferation of sects whose members were
still able to determine when they differed in opinion, is no
longer so applicable today. Even the most vehement Protestant attacks on Catholicism for its authoritarianism and
its antidemocratic tendencies are very often the result not
of any basic difference about the role of religion in national
life but of a sharp difference about whose religion is to
play that role.

To indicate the extent of this calculated Protestant authoritarianism, it will be sufficient to consider the role it
plays in: (1) the relations between clergy and laity within
the churches; and (2) the policies for public education advocated by many leading Protestants.

2 · *Limping Before the Lame*

Crane Brinton recently speculated that "the moral an-
guish of our age is rather the mark of the intellectual classes

in our West than of the many." [4] If the intellectual classes, like my Michigan companion, do not know what they are doing as they "watch the sun go down," the nonintellectual classes rarely get to know that the sun is descending. In the foreword to the 1946 edition of *Brave New World*, Aldous Huxley wrote:

> The greatest triumphs of propaganda have been accomplished, not by doing something, but by refraining from doing. . . . By simply not mentioning certain subjects, by lowering . . . an "iron curtain" between the masses and such facts or arguments as the local political bosses regard as undesirable, totalitarian propagandists have influenced opinion much more effectively than they could have by the most eloquent denunciations, the most compelling of logical rebuttals.

Contemporary Protestant theologians have lowered a curtain of formulae between the mass of Protestants and the problems of Protestantism. And this policy has during the past few years led to a practice that—although in itself an old policy—is rather new in American Protestantism.

Perhaps Dostoevsky has portrayed the policy, and the questions it raises, most vividly. In 1881 the Russian novelist placed on the lips of Ivan Karamazov, an atheist, the famous legend of the Grand Inquisitor, Cardinal of Seville, who deceived his flock for their own sakes. According to

[4] Crane Brinton: A *History of Western Morals* (London: Weidenfeld and Nicolson; 1959), pp. 391 f.

Ivan's tale, Christ had reappeared in Seville and had been promptly imprisoned by the Inquisition. Late at night the Cardinal—whom Ivan describes as also an atheist—visits Christ in the dungeon in an attempt to defend before Him his suppression of intellectual and religious freedom in Spain. Describing the believers whom he and those who shared his priestcraft had deceived, the Cardinal insists:

> We shall show them that they are weak, that they are only pitiful children, but that childlike happiness is the sweetest of all. . . . And all will be happy, all the millions of creatures, except the hundred thousand sufferers who have taken upon themselves the curse of the knowledge of good and evil. Peacefully they will die, peacefully they will expire in Thy name, and beyond the grave they will find nothing but death. But we shall keep the secret, and for their happiness we shall allure them with the reward of heaven and eternity. . . . Judge us if Thou canst and darest. . . . I too prized the freedom with which Thou hast blessed men. . . . But I awakened and would not serve madness. I turned back and joined the ranks of those who have corrected Thy work.

Four hundred years after the Grand Inquisitor, and three quarters of a century after Dostoevsky, Tillich has endorsed a similar kind of priestcraft. Like the Grand Inquisitor, Tillich does not believe in the popular "God of theism," the God who answers prayer and offers men a life beyond the grave. Frequently he has emphasized the contrast between his own theology and faiths that hold to a more literal interpretation of the Biblical teachings. For instance, Tillich writes:

> The primitive period of individuals and groups consists in the inability to separate the creations of symbolic imagination from the facts which can be verified through observation and experiment. *This stage has a full right of its own and should not be disturbed, either in individuals or in groups, up to the moment when man's questioning mind breaks the natural acceptance of the mythological visions as literal.*[5]

Tillich contrasts this stage with:

> the second stage of literalism, the conscious one, which is aware of the questions but represses them, half consciously, half unconsciously. The tool of repression is usually an acknowledged authority with sacred qualities like the Church or the Bible, to which one owes unconditional surrender. *This stage is still justifiable, if the questioning power is very weak and can easily be answered.* It is unjustifiable if a mature mind is broken in its personal center by political or psychological methods, split in his unity, and hurt in his integrity.[6]

Tillich and the Grand Inquisitor seem agreed on a number of points. Both believe that it is better to let *innocent* ignorance prevail. When doubts arise in an individual, they leave it to his minister to decide whether his doubts are weak enough to be refuted, or whether he must be made

[5] *Dynamics of Faith*, p. 52. Italics are mine.
[6] Ibid., p. 53.

one of the "hundred thousand sufferers" who inhabit the inner circle of the broken myth. Tillich and the Inquisitor most clearly *disagree* over a positive program of enforced ignorance: Tillich would sponsor no inquisition.

I have not brought these two passages together either to condemn Tillich or to suggest that his motives are similar to the Inquisitor's. Much as Dostoevsky hated the Cardinal's policy, he could not help portraying him sympathetically as one who "all his life loved humanity." At least as much must be said for Tillich. Indeed, it is ironical that the suggestion of such a comparison could even arise; for in his intellectual autobiography Tillich specifically mentions his personal *fight* against the figure of the Grand Inquisitor as "a decisive element of my theological thought." [7]

Although it is easy enough to deplore such ideas, certain questions arise: Aren't such practices inevitable? Isn't Tillich's approach in fact the only *realistic* one? Must we not simply accept the fact that people are different in their capabilities, that most men are simply beyond the reaches of theological interpretation? On this level at least, isn't a breakdown of communication unavoidable?

These questions sound reasonable, and some of them may be answered affirmatively. Certainly Tillich is not alone in his opinions about them. Not long ago, the late British philosopher C. E. M. Joad raised similar points. "Is it wise," he asked, "to continue to erode the foundations in history and metaphysics upon which the Christian faith is based? If we can't accept them ourselves, may it not, nevertheless,

[7] "Autobiographical Reflections," in *The Theology of Paul Tillich*, ed. Kegley and Bretall (New York: The Macmillan Company; 1956), p. 8.

be well that we should at least pretend, remembering in our emergency Plato's hint about the social beneficence of the useful lie?" [8]

Professor Huston Smith, of the Massachusetts Institute of Technology, has specifically defended Tillich's position with similar arguments. Every great historical religion, Smith argued, has a "layered character." "Indian thought," he points out, "has never hesitated to commend to persons at different levels of understanding different concepts of God, ranging from graven images to the absolutely formless Nirguna Brahman." Smith contends that although Western theology has allowed "less latitude," it too has accepted the principle. He gives as an example an old story about St. Thomas Aquinas: "When an old woman asked St. Thomas whether the names of all the blessed were written on a scroll exhibited in Heaven, he wrote back with untiring calm: 'So far as I can see this is not the case; but there is no harm in saying so.' " There is, Smith blandly concludes, no duplicity in this activity; it is simply founded on a basic fact about human nature.[9] Christ's wisdom, once unattainable to the wise and prudent and best available to the simple and to babes, has undergone a curious reversal.

Such "benevolent sowing of ignorance," like many other theological practices today, has a philosophical justification in the new Protestantism. Professor Smith's idea of a "layered truth" is in many respects an *internal* application of the notion of "truth for the committed group" which

[8] As quoted by Brand Blanshard in "The Morality of Self Respect," *The New Republic*, February 28, 1955.

[9] Smith made these remarks in a letter to *Harper's* which appeared in the section "Protestant Voices," July 1959.

has helped the theologians justify their general commitment vis-à-vis the wider external culture.

Yet, as Joad's remark suggests, Smith might have gone far back in the Western tradition, to one of its most respected sources, to find further justification for his position. He could have resorted to Plato's famous policy of "the royal lie," described in *The Republic* and *The Laws*, which allows the rulers, for the good of the state, to introduce certain myths designed to arrest social change and mobility. All that is really needed, Plato suggests, is "just one royal lie." [1] However, the great philosopher who immortalized Socrates' quest for truth explains *his* royal fib with some embarrassment—considerably more than Tillich, Smith, or even, apparently, St. Thomas, in his "untiring calm," seemed to show. "Well then," Plato says, "I will speak, although I really know not how to look you in the face, or in what words to utter the audacious fiction, which I propose to communicate gradually."

Hidden persuasion, then, is an old art. Yet Tillich's program cannot be explained by anything so simple as a "desire to deceive," or to arrest social change. Quite the contrary. The trouble with Tillich, as contrasted with Plato, is that Tillich's policy is not founded on a very realistic interpretation of human nature: his policy is surprisingly naïve. For one becomes neither profound nor realistic by making the rather obvious observation that most men are not very bright. To judge the role of religion, one must heed the logic of the situations in which the traditional religious stories are told today.

[1] Plato: *Republic*, 3, 414.

Such caution is particularly important for anyone who, like Tillich, plays the part of a "physician of society," a cultural psychiatrist who is concerned to "break the hold" of misleading "models" that are causing societal neurosis. Although one of the chief concerns of psychiatry is *preventative* medicine, Tillich and similar thinkers often attack neurosis—if they treat it at all—only *after* it has arisen. The question arises whether Tillich—by urging that the Christian myths be taught to unsophisticated people as "the truth," by encouraging children to acquire a literal understanding of them, and by arguing that this kind of religion is "justifiable" as long as no one is being *forced* to think this way—is not really, but of course unwittingly, spreading the seeds of conflict.

Consider the possible biography of a believer. Having been taught Bible stories as the truth in his nondoubting period, he grows up a devout believer. Then he reads a book or goes away to college and learns about the difficulties in religious belief. The resulting conflict may jeopardize not only his belief but his mental balance as well. His whole scheme of values may totter and fall. Before this point, ideally, the Tillichian minister comes along, asks a few astute questions to determine just how strong the doubt is, learns that the fellow's doubts cannot be quashed, and so reveals to him that the Christian stories are *really* symbolically true. "They are symbols, no less," the preacher says. "Didn't you know *that?* Why, that's what I meant all the time." The wise and realistic farmer need not destroy his own harvest.

The problem, of course, is a general one:

A diseased state of an organism, a society or culture, is characterized by a weakening of the integrative controls, and the tendency of its parts to behave in an independent and self-assertive manner, ignoring the superior interest of the whole, or trying to impose their own laws on it." [2]

Part of Tillich's mistake here was to let his love and often deep understanding of the Christian stories and traditions blind him to the daily tragedy of not-so-simple men who are shattered by the discovery that the creeds in which they put their trust are false and by the obvious inference they tend to make that *everything*, their whole world, is breaking down. Perhaps theologians will some day ponder how much of the mental disorder and meaninglessness that they say is prevalent among young people today is due to their discovery in late adolescence that the "true" Biblical stories they learned in their youth are literally false, and to their being accustomed from early childhood and from many traditions of Western culture to a peculiar *standard* of "ultimate satisfaction" and "ultimate meaning" that is both psychologically unrealistic and philosophically untenable.

But suppose it *were* realistic to think that ignorance could be sown benevolently and successfully by the representatives of Protestantism or of some other ideologically oriented group, in some "brave new America" of the future. Every would-be Protestant theologian must still answer for himself the question whether he intends to participate in such deception, however benevolent it might be.

[2] Koestler: *The Sleepwalkers*, p. 517.

Even if Tillich's main fault here was in fact lack of realism—perhaps a kind of social blindness linked with the dismal failure of the "religious socialism" he tried to lead to political power in Germany during the 1920's—he still cannot entirely be excused from the charge of having yielded to an old temptation that seems especially seductive to intellectuals: the urge to take it upon oneself to decide what is best for other people; the willingness to keep other people unconscious in order to prevent them from making errors. Perhaps this is an especially grave mistake for a Protestant theologian. For it involves a social policy that seems quite at variance with at least one of the traditional conceptions of Protestantism—the idea of the priesthood of all believers. According to a common interpretation of this idea, each man can and should seek out God for himself; no man is *dependent* on the intermediary activity of a church or priest, although he may, if he wishes, make use of such intermediaries. When joined, as it often has been, with the more obviously rationalized idea of the Quest, this principle has been one of the most important and fruitful concepts in the development of Western spiritual traditions. Together, the two ideas have nourished the belief in the importance of the individual human being. Here, the *quest* for God becomes most important for the individual, and it really does not matter greatly if someone on his own comes to a "wrong" conception of God. It may be immaterial that an old lady thinks the names of the blessed are exhibited on a scroll in heaven; or that someone else devotes his life to discovering whether angels are able to read and write. But it can be very serious if someone who believes that the names of the blessed are not so exhibited, or that there are no angels anyway, leads other gullible people, for his own purposes, to believe that there is such a heavenly exhibition—or that angels are literate. Protestantism, then, seems lost in the business of selling a product, whereas the quest for truth is something that can be neither sold nor bought.

To search after truth is to start to scale a mountain of infinite height. It is no more possible that some climber will reach the top than it is that some mathematician will count all the numbers. Yet, at least from the foothills below, the more distant reaches seem infinitely attractive. The visible snowcaps seem bathed in sunlight; and who knows what wonders are beyond the clouds? Most men go climbing at least for a while—with or without equipment and preparation, with or without natural strength.

Some of the most talented climbers have always been disappointed, soul-chillingly disappointed, on reaching the first snowcaps. It looked so much better from down below; and the climb itself was far more satisfying than the plateau. The mountain winds are real and cold, and the warmth of the sunlight is only an illusion. Self-pity often sets in—the self-pity that flees from itself to pity others. "The poor people down below!" the story goes. "They are really better off where they are, while they still have such great expectations." And so the people on the plateau set up a cloud factory to slow up the others for their own sake.

> *You are good when you walk to your goal*
> *firmly and with bold steps.*
> *Yet you are not evil when you go thither*
> *limping.*

Even those who limp go not backward.
But you who are strong and swift, see
that you do not limp before the
lame, deeming it kindness.[3]

3 · *The Educational Unifiers*

It is difficult to become very excited about the personal
ideological and spiritual tyranny, deplorable as it is, which
goes on within the church. Religious affiliation is voluntary;
and throughout much of the Western world an individual is
able to criticize the church before any audience whose attention he can gain. Besides, there are worse terrors in the
world than a tyranny of holy words to which one owes
obeisance whether or not they are rationally interpretable.
This situation begins to grow dangerous in the uncritical
attitude toward authority which it can encourage. If it is in
the "unswept corners of our intellectual universe that the
germs of epidemics are often bred," [4] an attempt to sweep
some of the usually skirted corners may be worthwhile.

There are many such germs in *education* today, often
sown by men who, frustrated and battered by the present,
would like to try to control the future by conditioning the
young people who will comprise it. One example of the
call to national ideological unity through the educational
system appeared in 1956, in a paper the Christian philosopher John Wild, then of Harvard University, delivered to a

[3] Kahlil Gibran: *The Prophet* (New York: Alfred A. Knopf; 1948), pp.
73 f.

[4] E. H. Gombrich: *Art and Scholarship*, Inaugural Lecture delivered at
University College, London (London: H. K. Lewis & Co.; 1957), p. 14.

conference at the Harvard School of Education.[5] Wild attributed many of the troubles of the West to its lack of a unified educational structure and insisted that just such a structure "is the most desperate need of our time." Claiming that the great contemporary world cultures—his examples are Buddhism, Hinduism, Mohammedanism, and the Marxism-Leninism of the U.S.S.R.—"are guided by overarching patterns of religious and philosophic thought which are cultivated in their schools, and which elicit voluntary devotion," Wild called attention to the roots of Russian culture in the philosophy of Marx's teacher Hegel:

> This semi-religious philosophy has been corrected and refined by several generations of thinkers, including Marx and Lenin. At the present time it includes fundamental ontology based on evidence accessible to all which can give an intelligible account of the results of the different sciences, a philosophy of man and human history which takes account of many facts, an ethics which claims to be grounded in the dialectic laws of nature, and a penetrating analysis of class conflict which has already offered unequivocal guidance for social action, and which has a profound appeal to many scientific minds, and to millions of oppressed people all over the world. Hence it is no accident that this integrating culture is far more formidable than any other now confronting us. The view of the world which binds it together is taught as a compulsory subject in every

[5] "Philosophy of Education in the West: A Desperate Present Need," *The Harvard Educational Review*, 1956. See Wild's letter to *The New Republic*, May 5, 1958, p. 12, and my reply, *The New Republic*, May 19, 1958.

Russian high school as well as in every technical school and university. What do we have in the West corresponding to this great overarching structure of ideas? What integrating view of the world now guides our Western life and policy? . . . There is none!

One might prod Professor Wild's statement in many places, beginning with a few questions about this "compulsory subject" which elicits such "voluntary devotion." Such criticism is unnecessary here. Wild's address was only an especially excited version of a point of view one often encounters in Protestant as well as Catholic discussions about the place of religion in higher education: in Sir Walter Moberly's *Crisis in the University*; in Henry P. Van Dusen's *God in Education*; in George A. Buttrick's *Faith and Education*; in Howard Lowry's *The Mind's Adventure*; in T. S. Eliot's *The Idea of a Christian Society*; in the Kent School Symposium on *The Christian Idea of Education*.

Broadly stated, the view diagnoses that in order to destroy the Western tower of Babel, its self-doubt, hesitation, anxiety, lack of effective communication, and disagreement, the West needs to adopt a comprehensive cultural ideology—usually some form of Christianity. Very few advocates of such views suggest Communist-type enforcement of their "overarching faith." Certainly Wild does not. Most, like Wild, give no directions at all, indulging in a latter-day "belling of the cat." A few, to be sure, have been somewhat more explicit. In his book *Christ and Man's Dilemma*,[6] George A. Buttrick, the former chaplain to Har-

[6] George A. Buttrick: *Christ and Man's Dilemma* (Nashville: Abingdon Press), Chap. VI.

vard, argued that "an agreed-upon syllabus of religious studies" should be instituted in the American public-school system. But if it were impossible to achieve such a syllabus, Buttrick proceeded, very seriously, to argue:

> it would be better—however unfortunate and schismatic—for each faith to build its own schools rather than continue with a merely secular education. . . . I hold the conviction regarding Protestant denominations that, however worthy and heroic their respective origins, the crisis of our time now requires their unity. So deep is this conviction that I suspect the phrase "unity, not uniformity," for I wonder how there can be unity without *some* clear form, since unity cannot be a disembodied spirit. The tragic dismemberment of Protestantism is more tragic because it cripples Protestantism in its task of real education. A united Protestantism could help offset the blight of secularism in education; a dismembered Protestantism is a tragedy, and may now be a crime. But, if secular education is to remain merely secular, any substitute in truer basic faith, even though I would deplore a dismembered substitute, would be a gain. . . . By whatever worthy means, at the price of whatever temporary chaos, secular education must become religious, or the religious community must establish its own schools.[7]

[7] For an illustration of such worthy means and temporary chaos in action, see the literature relating to the religious controversy at Harvard University, March and April 1958, beginning with my article "Religion at Harvard," *Harvard Crimson*, March 28, 1958 (reprinted in *The New Republic*, April 21, 1958). Several paragraphs in the text above are paraphrased from this article. See also the almost daily correspondence about this matter printed in the *Crimson* during April 1958, and the

Similar ideas about how American education might combat secularism in a more unified way—"at the price of whatever temporary chaos"—appeared in some remarks made by a Catholic, Father John Courtney Murray, at the predominantly Protestant Kent School Symposium:

> We have the older students in the college and the university. Shouldn't it be possible to make an impact upon their imaginations with the humanities and with Christian doctrine in such wise that we would, as it were, immunize them from the impact of the scientific experience?

Students would also be immunized, apparently, from the disintegrating effects of intelligent reflection and searching examination. Moberly, for instance, has written:

> In Europe amoralism is widely prevalent; and our own abler young men will accept nothing from tradition without searching examination. We academic people are too little awake to this disintegration. . . .

In this flip way, searching examination of oneself and one's tradition, activities that have, at least since the time of Socrates, stamped man as civilized, are pronounced marks of disintegration.

Many questions reaching far beyond the bounds of educational theory arise out of the various proposals of unification. Two of the most important are: Does the West need a common faith in its battle with Communism? And if so,

---

reports of the controversy and its results which appeared in *The St. Louis Post-Dispatch*, May 11, 1958; *Harvard Crimson*, April 23, 1958; and *Time*, April 14, 1958.

is this faith Christianity? It is practically impossible to answer the second question affirmatively. There are too many different Christianities for Christianity to act as a system that Western men might agree on today, whatever its unifying power half a millennium ago. Moreover, it is difficult to see how any Protestant theologian who maintains that any future intellectual synthesis, when and if it does come, must be a Christian synthesis can escape being justly accused of precisely the sort of intellectual pride that Protestant theologians so automatically deplore when it appears among non-Christians.

An approach toward an answer to the first question is available in James Bryant Conant's book *The Citadel of Learning*. There Conant gives a critique of Soviet education which serves almost as a point-by-point rebuttal of the kind of theory many of the contemporary Christian unifiers espouse. Writing of some of his experiences as American ambassador to the Federal Republic of West Germany, Conant noted that no one "uses the word 'unity' more frequently than those who are attempting to force the Soviet ideology on the people of the Russian zone." Their educational syllogism, he states, goes like this: Education is concerned with truth, truth is everywhere the same, therefore education should be everywhere the same. Pointing out the pernicious effects of such a doctrine in practice, as in the Lysenko case, for example, Conant argues that a scientist or a scholar, to the degree that he is dedicated to the advancement of learning as such, must aim to contribute to a long-range human enterprise, not to an immediate undertaking or battle. "If anyone in the free world believes that a unifying philosophy is a goal to be desired at whatever

price," Conant suggests, "then he should drive from the free
sectors of Berlin eastward through the Brandenburg Gate."
The words "at whatever price"—recalling Buttrick's
phrase "at the price of whatever temporary chaos"—
should be underscored. For some Protestant philosophers of
education apparently are willing to unify the curriculum at
whatever price. So distinguished and genuinely liberal a
Christian educator as Henry P. Van Dusen, president of
Union Theological Seminary, a charter member of the
Board of Trustees of Princeton University, has written:

> Instructors might protest that, if they were adequately
> to teach their several subjects in conformity to the
> basic premise of the Unity of Truth, they would be
> compelled to recast the underlying structure of their
> minds. To which it might be replied, perhaps that is
> just what is required, if they are to fulfill their central
> loyalty to Truth.

One wonders how the recasting of the "underlying structure" of one's mind differs from brainwashing. Since it is
structural, perhaps it is meant to be more thorough than
mere washing. And, of course, the "compelling" would
doubtless be voluntary.

These calls for ideological unity often reflect a desire that
society have the symmetry and internal order of a painting,
a formula, a building. When juxtaposed with some other
themes of contemporary Protestantism, however, such aes-
theticism evokes a special irony. For one of the soundest
distinctions made popular by this theology is that between
the "I," the "thou," and the "it"—a distinction which the

theologians have used in deploring the "scientific" practice of treating man as an *object* instead of as a *subject*. Yet what objectifies man more than the attempt to paint him fast and predictably into the order of a social canvas? [8]

[8] Compare T. S. Eliot: *The Idea of a Christian Society* (New York: Harcourt, Brace and Company; 1940), p. 26; and Aldous Huxley: *Brave New World* (London: Penguin Books; 1955), Chap. XVII.

EPILOGUE

THE LEADING Protestant theologians of the twentieth century have, then, embraced as fact the philosophical contention that rationality is logically limited, that every man—will he, nill he—makes some ultimately irrational commitment; and they have used this contention to excuse rationally their own irrational commitment to Christ. Thereby, they have been able in principle, although not in practice, to avoid loss of intellectual integrity.

I have tried to refute the philosophical theory about the limits of rationality by turning the tables, by showing how we can shift the emphasis in rational discussion from justification to a nonjustificational criticism of our beliefs and commitments. I hope, in this way, to have helped clarify the issues of identity and integrity in both Protestantism and rationalism, and to have made the choice at least clearer to individuals who are torn between them. If my argument is sound, there can no longer be a general rational excuse for ultimate irrational commitments. Those who continue to make them will *really* be irrationalists, in the sense that they will not be able to retain their Protestant identity with the intellectual integrity which the argument about the limits of rationality afforded them, so long as it went unrefuted.

Still, my argument does not force anyone to be a rationalist; it only shows that there is no rational or logical excuse for being an irrationalist. Anyone who wishes, or who is personally able to do so, may remain an irrationalist. And it may be difficult indeed to argue with any such person, for he will have abandoned argument. No one, for instance, can expect to convince the neurotic that he is ill if he cannot or will not accept the diagnosis. The person who fervently believes that one is equal to zero need never admit that two and two equal four. I cannot convince a man like Hitler that murder is wrong. And I hardly know where to begin arguing with the Anglican canon who announced in 1958 that mental patients are not ill but are *really* possessed by evil spirits. Doubtless they are, at least symbolically speaking.

How should a man who is trying to be a rationalist act toward such people? If the rationalist were in fact *committed* to rationalism, he would be entitled to treat such people as they treat him: he could regard them as members of a different *ecclesia*, or ultimately committed religious community, whom—since real argument was impossible—he could best hope to convert through nonrational persuasion.

But since the rationalist, as I have tried to show, need be committed neither to his rationalism nor to any other of his beliefs, he need not repudiate people with whom he fundamentally disagrees. In principle, he can act toward them in a remarkable way.

In the old story, the Pennsylvania Dutchman says to his wife: "Everybody is crazy but me and thee, Hanna, and sometimes I wonder even about thee."

Anybody, from the neurotic to Reinhold Niebuhr, can play Pennsylvania Dutchman and ask us to "take the leap of faith"—whether it is a "great leap forward," a great leap backward, or a somersault on the *status quo*—to his own irrational commitment. That commitment may carry consolations; there are, as Ibsen knew, such things as "saving lies." But if we look before we leap—and when the chasm is very wide, he who hesitates is not necessarily lost—many of us will be unable to crucify our intellects without impaling our integrity.

As long as the *tu quoque* argument about the limits of rationality stood unchallenged, it was possible for a man to crucify his intellect, to make an irrational commitment, without impaling his integrity. For those who claimed to be rationalists had clearly impaled *their* integrity. However, having discovered why that argument is invalid, I no longer need to make that leap; and I do not think anyone else has to do so either. People can, like Lessing, be engaged without being committed.[1]

Yet anyone who has grappled with the arguments about ultimate commitment and the limits of rationality, and who has appreciated what a strong case the irrationalists have been able to put up, should have acquired at least one virtue: a measure of intellectual humility. For rationalists can and very often do make mistakes, too. I used to think the best approach in almost any disagreement (provided none of the disputants had the power to impose his opinions in the way Hitler did) was one that my former teacher at

[1] See E. H. Gombrich's fascinating account in his "Lessing, Lecture on a Master Mind," *Proceedings of the British Academy*, 1957. (Oxford: Oxford University Press; 1958).

Harvard, Professor Morton White, once imaginatively rec-
ommended by endorsing Hamlet's reply to the Queen:

> *My pulse, as yours, doth temperately keep time,*
> *And makes as healthful music. It is not madness*
> *That I have uttered. . . .*
>   *. . . Mother, for love of grace,*
> *Lay not that flattering unction to your soul,*
> *That not your trespass, but my madness speaks!*

Although I still think Hamlet's advice is sound, I have
altered my attitude toward it. The would-be comprehensive
rationalist, as I once was, usually presumes that his opponent is a fool. For the self-conscious comprehensive rationalist knows in his heart that his own position is riddled with
inconsistencies, and "whoever is hard put to feel identical
with one set of people and ideas must that much more
violently repudiate another set." [2] Hence, I used to picture
myself self-righteously repeating Hamlet's words to those
who practiced the "queen of the sciences." Today, more
secure in a comprehensively *critical* rationalism which
makes no claims that it cannot carry through, which recog-
nizes that although rationality is indeed unlimited we are
all nonetheless prone to error, that "while differing widely
in the various little bits we know, in our infinite ignorance
we are all equal," [3] I try to imagine my opponents reciting
Hamlet's passage back to me; and I try to listen to it as good
advice for me, *as well as for them.*

Such an attitude, which helps us to treat our opponents

[2] Erikson: *Young Man Luther*, p. 259.
[3] Popper: "On the Sources," op. cit., p. 70.

as sane men, or perhaps simply as *men*, and which is rooted
in the admission that "I may be wrong and you, even you, a
poor irrationalist, may be right," makes argument, and
learning—scientific, moral, metaphysical, and religious—
possible. For each of us plays Pennsylvania Dutchman at
some time of his life. And sometimes the Pennsylvania
Dutchman is right.

Perhaps surprisingly, the practice of asking one's opponents for criticisms of one's own position, and of taking
these criticisms seriously, resembles in certain ways a Christian position. It recalls the Sermon-on-the-Mount idea of
turning the other cheek, and this resemblance, however
faint, leads to some interesting reflections.

When Jesus, in his Sermon, admonished his listeners to
turn the other cheek and go the second mile, he probably
had in mind practical human relationships. The exegetical
problem of whether his suggestions were intended to apply
only to a short period preceding the imminent coming of
the Kingdom of God, or to a longer period, does not arise
here. What is important is that few people today would put
much faith in such utopian policies. They have learned too
much from the times and from recent moralists, both
Protestant and secular, to treat the Sermon on the Mount
as a rule book for practical politics.

The situation is somewhat different if one applies the
Sermon's injunctions not to politics but to the business of
argument and discussion. Where argument about the world
and discussion of problems are concerned, some of the
advice contained in the Sermon on the Mount is highly
realistic. Perhaps this is not so surprising as it might sound

in isolation—or even in the present context. For if we treat
our opponents in discussion *not as they treat us, but as we
would have them treat us,* it is we who profit. When our
object is to learn rather than to win a debate, we must take
our opponents' arguments seriously and not reject them
unless we can refute them. As far as our aim, learning about
the world and ourselves, is concerned, it does not matter
whether our opponent reciprocates, or whether he treats our
own arguments as no more than emotive signals. We may
learn from the criticisms of our opponents even when their
own practice prevents them from learning from us. Whatever his real motive or intention may be, the rationalist
acts in his own interest (provided his interest is learning)
when he takes his opponents' thoughts seriously, when he
treats his opponent as a person rather than as a tiresome
talking machine he would like to switch off.

This is not to say that such an ethic can be properly
applied to every argument situation. For example, it would
be clearly wrong to replace the adversary system of our law
courts with it. However, when our aim is to answer religious
problems, it is pointless to overstate our claims, as it were,
to make sure that we are awarded satisfactory damages.

I have mentioned this parallel not in order to come back
to Christianity through the attic window, but to point out
yet another irony in the new theology. When it comes to
critical discussion, those who divide the world into "us" and
"they," appeal to the so-called limits of rationality and the
necessity of commitment, and then preach to their opponents rather than argue with them, at once forget their own
advice and also fail to use one of the most appealing features
of Christianity—the Sermon on the Mount—in one of the

very few practical contexts in which it may occasionally be appropriate.

The last, but far from imaginary, opponent whose arrows I shall face before closing is no cupid, though he speaks in the name of love.

My position, he will say, is far removed from any religion of love. The comprehensively critical rationalism I have championed, he will add, is a ruthless policy that replaces loving commitment with cold scrutiny. For the relationship of commitment is like the relationship of love. We do not argue ourselves into love, and once in love we do not try to argue ourselves out again. No one who loves truly will deliberately subject his loved ones to danger. But criticism may be dangerous; to subject our love commitments to criticism is therefore to endanger them. By advocating comprehensively critical rationalism, I advocate a harsh cruel attitude unworthy of sensitive and civilized men. Love *should* be blind.

In an unloving world, the ability to love is a precious talent, and not just because it is rare. If certain people have nothing better to love than some idea—or perhaps a fancy about a prophet who lived and died long ago, leaving traces so scanty and conflicting that some of his most dedicated modern biographers say that we can know little of what he was like or what he did—who can condemn such people? Let them love when and what they can.

But what a sorry kind of love. Love is not for ideas but for individual people, real and alive, and—already in a different sense—for our live and vivid memories of people we once loved directly.

And what a dangerous kind of love. For when the love of ideas and fancies becomes a substitute for the love of living people, the lover, the committed man, often subordinates the requirements of human beings to the claims of his idea —the "demand of the object." Thus, that most inhuman of transformations occurs: human beings become objects, to be bent, broken, molded, even "educated," for the love of an idea.

There is yet another and still more important objection to the would-be spokesman for love. Although I have suggested that a sound ethic for argument could be read into Jesus' words in the Sermon on the Mount, I did not intend that ethic as an endorsement of Christianity or as a divine sanction for comprehensively critical rationalism or, most important, as part of a religion of love. Too many people who do not love anyone in particular like to talk grandly about their love for humanity. If anything, there is too much rather than too little of this love of humanity in the world today. Such talk of love, which can cover almost any sentiment or policy, suggests the danger and difficulty, if not the impossibility, of attempting to spread love too widely, of trying to make it into a universal religion. Love should not be treated like a commodity: offered to a few people with lavished care, it can flourish and return itself beyond expectation; but anyone who pretends to offer it to all comers at once misrepresents himself and turns his would-be gift into a mass product.

The ethic of argument that I endorse invokes a different sort of sentiment, which can be spread far more widely: *respect* for people. Whether one owes love to few people or many, one owes respect to all—at least until they very definitely show themselves unworthy of it. One of the most important ways of indicating *prima facie* respect for a person is to attempt to take his views seriously. This would be impossible if rationality were so limited that critical argument was impossible. I have tried in this essay to promote this sort of respect by showing that the critical argument it calls for is possible and by illustrating some of the unfortunate consequences of the retreat to commitment.

Index

A NOTE ON THE TYPE

THIS BOOK is set in ELECTRA, a Linotype face designed by W. A. Dwiggins (1880–1956). This face cannot be classified as either modern or old-style. It is not based on any historical model, nor does it echo any particular period or style. It avoids the extreme contrasts between thick and thin elements that mark most modern faces, and attempts to give a feeling of fluidity, power, and speed.

Composed, printed, and bound by
Kingsport Press, Inc., Kingsport, Tennessee.
Typography and binding design based
on originals by
W. A. DWIGGINS

WILLIAM WARREN BARTLEY III, who was born near Pittsburgh in 1934, received his A.B. from Harvard College in 1956. He continued his studies at Harvard's Divinity School, Law School, and Graduate School of Arts and Sciences, receiving an A.M. from the latter in 1958. In that year he went to England as a Fulbright Scholar, and completed his studies for the Ph.D degree at the London School of Economics and Political Science, where he was appointed Lecturer in Logic in 1960. Since October 1961 he has been Lecturer in the History of the Philosophy of Science at the Warburg Institute of the University of London. Mr. Bartley has been a reporter for the *Boston Globe* and is at present associate editor of the scholarly journal *History and Theory*. He has contributed to a number of publications including *The New Republic, Commentary, The British Journal for the Philosophy of Science, Philosophical Studies,* and *Harper's,* where the appearance of his article, "I Call Myself a Protestant," in 1959, stirred a great deal of controversy and ultimately led to the writing of this book.

January 1962